MARY ZICAFOOSE

ikat

the essential handbook to weaving resist-dyed cloth

Interweave

Interweave
An imprint of Penguin Random House LLC
penguinrandomhouse.com

 Interweave®

Printed in China
1 3 5 7 9 10 8 6 4 2

ISBN 978-1-63250-678-8

EDITORIAL DIRECTOR: Kerry Bogert
EDITOR: Nathalie Mornu
EDITORIAL COORDINATOR: Hayley DeBerard
TECHNICAL EDITOR: Catharine Ellis
COVER DESIGNER: Ashlee Wadeson
INTERIOR BOOK DESIGN: Tara Long
ILLUSTRATOR: Deanna Deeds
COVER PHOTOGRAPHY: Mary Zicafoose
PROCESS PHOTOGRAPHY: Jeffrey Hahn
PROJECT PHOTOGRAPHY: Matt Graves
STYLING: Ann Swanson and Nathalie Mornu

contents

Scrap of Indonesian ikat fabric,
given to the author by her aunt.

INTRODUCTION

I fell in love with ikat as a child after a favorite aunt gifted me a scrap of fabric, a travel souvenir from Indonesia. Instinctively I knew there was something very unusual about this cloth. I was enchanted with the finely feathered edges where the vibrant dyes seeped and resisted. This was a magical fabric, more about narrative art than utilitarian object—a small section of an ancient story, holding mystery and delight. Years later a prophetic incident occurred during a college portfolio critique, enlivening my memory of that exotic fabric. My design professor informed me that my work in two-dimensional media was desperately trying to become a textile. My use of pattern reminded her of a very distinct and graphic type of ethnic cloth. Leaving the review, she handed me a slip of paper scrawled with the word "IKAT."

Often, we don't recognize forks in the road. I don't recall making a conscious decision to "become" a weaver, yet I always knew that I would one day unlock the secret to the magic contained within that scrap of childhood cloth. My instincts were correct. My early fascination led me full circle into the arms of the ancient resist-wrap process called ikat.

Everything I know about ikat I've learned through trial and error. I haven't studied at the feet of an ikat master. In fact, I've never taken an ikat workshop. I'm not descended from a long lineage of ethnic ikat weavers, nor do I live in a part of the world revered for its production of ikat cloth. All that I'm sharing with you has been learned and tested over many years in the studio creating weft-ikat tapestries and rugs. The ikat techniques that I practice are adapted and refined through my personal lens, the interpretation of an American artist who weaves.

This book provides an introduction to ikat techniques through a selection of nine projects that teach aspects of warp, weft, and double ikat. It does not provide instruction in beginning weaving. I am assuming the reader has experience winding a warp, warping a loom, and weaving yarns into cloth. Each project sequentially illustrates a new ikat skill set, either in design, yarn management, resist-wrapping, dyeing, or weaving. Whether you're a beginning weaver or quite advanced, the project format—a long narrow rectangle—is a simple technical construction, beautifully showcasing ikat design while allowing you to express your personal style. I've included many technical tips, sketchbook notes, personal stories, and favorite images taken from three decades of my affair with ikat.

As with so many traditions, the story is never quite well told until the past has been recognized and respect paid. To accomplish this, I went straight to knowledgeable ikat sources. You will discover compelling stories tucked at the ends of chapters, shared by textile scholars, curators, and colleagues, each contributing their point of view about the unique cloth made in regions of the world significant in the history of ikat.

If you're striving to make your woven work appear more painterly and are intrigued by the ancient alchemy between color, elements, and spirit that happens within a dyepot, then ikat may be the pathway to a new adventure in textiles. This is a workbook combining cultural inspiration with classic projects that teach introductory ikat techniques.

CHAPTER ONE | what is ikat?

Is it possible that the movement of ikat across the globe was driven more by the quest for the mystical, rather than by the train of world events? As spices and goods moved along the Silk Road and sailed across oceans, so traveled scraps and lengths of this exotically embellished cloth. And just as I, as a young child, was startled by its mysteriously coded beauty, so, too, were the ancient camel driver, spice merchant, and weaver; all of us have been touched by the power of this cloth.

Ikat is the centuries-old art and technique of resist-dyeing pattern into threads before weaving. The term *ikat* originates from the Malay-Indonesian verb *mengikat*, which means to tie, bind, or wind around. The process is mathematical, exacting, and labor intensive, eventually rendering each strand of yarn coded and layered with pixels of imagery and color. Ikat is not a weave structure. You won't find books of patterns and weaving drafts containing plans for different ways of threading and treadling your loom to create ikat designs. The basic steps of the ikat process are virtually the same throughout the world.

1. Sections of warp and/or weft threads are counted, stretched, and held under consistent tension on a frame. Types and styles of tying frames vary greatly from country to country, the simplest being two stakes driven into the ground.

2. The stretched threads are marked in some manner, indicating which areas are to be tied and which areas are to remain uncovered, free to absorb the dye.

3. The marked sections of threads are bound and tied with a resist-wrapping material. Traditionally, this task has been accomplished using easily accessible materials that resist dye—dried grasses, vines, leaves, and in some parts of the world even bicycle inner tubes. Special tapes are now available that are suitable for wrapping fibers.

4. The wrapped sections are then dyed. All ikats made before the industrial revolution used natural dyes, indigo being a favorite source of blue. Today both synthetic and natural dye systems are popularly used worldwide.

Pulling and shifting threads during weaving can further emphasize the feathered and blurry edges of ikat.

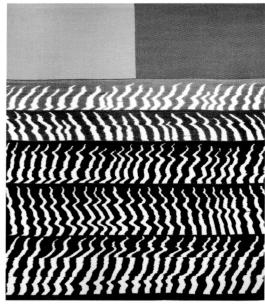

Mary Zicafoose, Fields of Desire, 2013, weft face ikat tapestry, 66 × 62" (168 × 157 cm), collection of Alley Poyner Macchietto Architecture, Omaha, NE, photo: Kirby Zicafoose

5. For complex designs requiring multiple colors, dyed threads are selectively unwrapped, restretched on the frame, rewrapped, and submerged in different color dyebaths. This exposes specific sections of the threads to a new dye color, while the previously dyed areas are wrapped and protected or completely overdyed.

6. Dyed yarns are unwrapped, dried, organized, and woven into ikat cloth.

The characteristic feathered and blurry edge of ikat is created by dye wicking up under the binding during the dye process. It can be further emphasized during weaving when threads are intentionally pulled and shifted.

In many parts of the world, each step in the elaborate ikat process is performed by a different skilled craftsman. The dyer does not wrap the yarn. The warp stretcher does not weave the cloth, and the designer is only responsible for pattern making. In ikat cultures in places such as India, Japan, Indonesia, and Central Asia, the resist-dyeing is considered the art form, not the weaving of the cloth. The over-and-under process that interlaces the ikat-dyed threads into cloth at the loom is only as important as a canvas is to a painter. The weaving is simply what holds all the color and pattern together. Historically, resist-dyed fabrics are revered and often carry deep symbolic meaning. They are the cloths of spirit, instrumental during rites of passage, ceremonies of ritual and faith, and events of great prestige.

Clothing and items made of dyed and woven ikat threads have always been considered precious and unique, commanding great respect. Despite its legendary complexity, the ikat technique is driven by one powerful intention: to produce a timeless, striking, and visually opulent textile.

Wendy Weiss, *Gaza, Scar, Camp*, 2018, warp ikat, warp dyed with ferrous fermentation vat, weft dyed with weld, handwoven on 20-shaft loom, photo: Jay Kreimer. This Nebraska weaver, who received two Fulbright fellowships to study ikat with master weavers in India, creates sculptural and very dimensional textured textiles, dramatically combining complex design and weave structures with warp ikat.

THE DIFFERENT TYPES OF IKAT

All ikat cloth is referred to as either warp ikat, weft ikat, double ikat, or compound ikat, depending on whether the resist binding is wrapped around groups of threads of the warp, the weft, or both. Warp ikat and weft ikat are two very different kinds of cloth, each requiring different methods of yarn management and design preparation, but both are woven using resist-wrapped and dyed yarns. Double ikat and compound ikat are a clever design combination using both the warp and weft systems. How you stretch, wrap, dye, warp, and weave the yarns is a practiced skill and the ikat art form. The specific step-by-step techniques to learn warp, weft, and double ikat are explained in detail through the projects taught in this book.

WARP IKAT

Traditionally, most ikats are plain-woven warp ikats. The vividness of an ikat pattern depends very much on the weave structure of the cloth, and especially on the balance between warp and weft. The most graphic and distinct warp-ikat patterns are achieved when the warp yarn dominates the weft. To create this effect, you'll generally select warp threads that are thicker and heavier than the weft or use fine warp yarns threaded in an extremely dense and close warp-faced sett on the loom.

The clearest ikat image resolution is most successfully achieved in a pure rep weave. This is a weave structure characterized by compacting four times the usual number of warp threads per inch or centimeter of warp. Warp-ikat designs also "pop" and show contrast quite vividly when woven as a satin weave or a warp-faced 3/1 or 2/1 twill. In many weave structures, portions of the weft yarn are visible, in varying degrees, minimizing the impact and stealing the thunder from the warp-ikat design.

Samples from the author's collection of global ikat cloth.

Wendy Weiss, *Red Diamonds*, cotton warp ikat dyed with madder root and weld. Inspired by ikat tiraz, Cleveland Museum of Art, photo: artist.

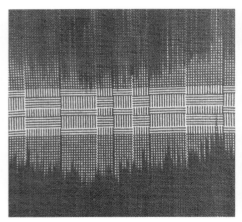

Catharine Ellis, *Ikat Log Cabin* (detail), 1992, cotton and fiber reactive dye, warp ikat on alternate warp threads to create log cabin effect, photo: artist.

Ikat in process on loom, Bukhara,
Uzbekistan, photo: Mary Zicafoose.

By definition, all ikat demands extra time and effort spent wrapping, dyeing, unwrapping, and organizing threads so they're ultimately coded with a design. If the goal is to show as much of the dyed threads as possible, why then would the weaver cover up the ikat design on a warp with a weft-faced weave or thick weft yarns? Weavers have always selected the fibers and setts that best show off their ikat designs.

The first projects presented in this book are warp ikat. The warp will be wrapped with resist tape while stretched on the warping board. This is a convenient process, but not all ideas for warp-ikat designs can be executed by wrapping the warp on the warping board. The warping board as a stretching tool works well for simple wrap projects but is sometimes not the right tool for more complex designs that require wrapping stretched yarns following a wrapping pattern (which I call a cartoon). One of the challenges for a beginning ikat weaver is to figure out a satisfactory method to stretch and prepare a long warp for wrapping once it's removed from the warping board. Guatemala is a country known for its ikat clothing and for its complicated "jaspe" (ikat) techniques. Long warps are often stretched in fields, streets, or courtyards, with one person standing at one end of a field holding the secured warp through a sectioned reed and their partner across the field holding the other end of the tensioned warp, with others assisting in the organizing, counting, dividing, wrapping, or unwrapping of fibers.

In many cultures, the long warp dilemma is managed by folding and doubling up warps on themselves for greater efficiency in handling and wrapping.

Methods and tips for stretching and managing long warps off the warping board are covered on page 35.

Unwrapping a long Guatemalan ikat warp stretched across a field, photo: Joe Coca.

A Guatemalan ikat weaver setting up her warp-ikat stretching system, photo: Joe Coca.

Securing a section of warp to begin resist-binding by master weaver Vitthalbhai Vaghela, who lives in the Surendranagar area of Gujarat, India. The long warp has been folded in half and then in half again, photo: Vitthalbhai Vaghela.

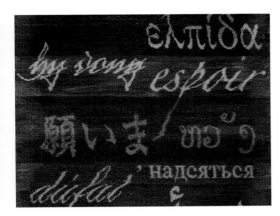

Mary Zicafoose, *The Hope Tapestry* (detail), 2017,
weft-face ikat tapestry triptych, 124 × 100" (315 × 254 cm),
Fred & Pamela Buffet Cancer Center, Omaha, NE, photo: Kirby Zicafoose.

Beth Ross Johnson, *At the Fell of the Sea 1*, 2014, shifted weft ikat,
6-harness satin weave, cotton warp, silk weft, fiber reactive dyes,
20 × 20" (51 × 51 cm), photo: Tim Barnwell.

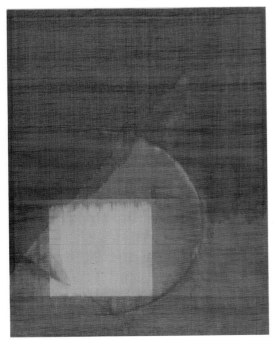

WEFT IKAT

Weft ikat is a less common version of ikat cloth. It's a different kind of a complicated process. In addition to the standard yarn stretching, resist-wrapping, and dyeing tasks, one must also deal with the cloth selvedges as part of the design and weaving consideration. In some types of weft ikat, the design created on the resist-dyed weft threads registers back on itself continuously and accurately with each shot as you weave. Depending on the project, and if you calculated correctly, the weft will form two uniform and beautiful cloth selvedges, as well.

Why and in what type of projects would you use weft ikat? There are several different approaches to answering this question. One approach generally employs the use of thick resist-wrapped yarns, and another usually showcases fine thin ikat-dyed threads.

The thick-yarn, weft-faced approach applies to projects that maximize and showcase the weft, such as rugs, tapestries, some table linens, and wall hangings. Weft-face weaves usually employ a widely spaced warp, providing unseen structural support, featuring a completely dominant weft yarn that beats in tightly, completely covering the warp. In such projects, firm, even, and very straight selvedges are trademarks of well-measured and managed weft-ikat yarns. In my tapestry and ikat classes I teach students to weave selvedges that "look like God wove them." This metaphor suggests that beautifully aligned, neatly woven selvedges are divinely inspired.

The thin-yarn approach references Japanese ikat, *kasuri*. In this system, the fine patterned weft threads are shifted and manipulated by hand during weaving to fit together to create designs and pictures, called *yoko-kasuri*. The arranging of coded yarns into designs happens through manipulation at the loom, rather than precisely calculated measurement and wraps at the ikat boards. The weft yarns are often allowed to extend beyond the selvedges when necessary in order to assist in lining up and registering areas of ikat design precisely where they need to fall to complete a design or motif, such as a pictorial landscape, known as *e-kasuri*. This particular kind of ikat cloth can be used in clothing construction, like a kimono, so a selvedge with many weft threads hanging out isn't an issue, as that part of the cloth won't be seen—it can be cut off or sewn into the seam of a garment. Extending weft threads beyond the selvedge can also become part of the planned design and aesthetic of the piece of ikat cloth.

Polly Barton, *Thistledown,* 2016, double ikat, silk warp, silk and metallic
weft, Tinfix dye and vermillion sumi ink, photo: Wendy McEahern. Trained to
weave in Japan, the New Mexico artist uses single, double, and pictorial ikat
in her woven silk paintings.

Carol Cassidy, silk weft-ikat scarf, from the author's collection. Purchased in Laos.

Fine ikat-dyed threads can also be precisely used for a perfectly controlled selvedge in weft ikat. A masterful example of this is my all-time favorite ikat scarf, a gift from friends, purchased in Laos at the studio of the American weaver Carol Cassidy. Very fine silk threads are used for both warp and weft. The gold zig-zag ikat patterning is wrapped and dyed on the weft threads, which are woven in precise sequence, with the design falling perfectly onto itself, as well as forming perfect selvedges. It appears to be woven effortlessly, with a beautiful hand and drape to the cloth, as if the ikat design just slipped into place and built up with every shot of weaving—with no matching or registering required.

DOUBLE IKAT

Double ikat is created by patterned warp and weft threads precisely intersecting with each other to form or complete a design/image such as a cross. True double-ikat cloth is a textile wonder of the world. It's considered a sacred practice, very carefully taught and maintained in only a handful of towns and villages in India, Indonesia, and Asia that specialize in the very labor-intensive and complex technique.

American weavers Virginia Davis and Polly Barton are articulate artists and masters at double ikat. Davis, of Berkeley, CA, has studied traditional ikat techniques from many cultures and makes use of these as well as ones she has developed in her work.

COMPOUND & RANDOM-WEFT IKAT

If patterned warp and weft yarns are laid in randomly, with no intention of creating a precise intersection, the process is simply called compound ikat. Random-weft ikats are created by combining unmatched ikat components, often borrowed from different projects.

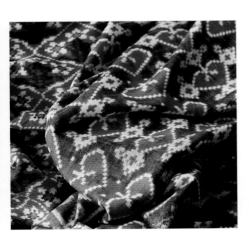

Indian double-ikat cloth,
photo: Maiwa School of Textiles, Tim McLaughlin.

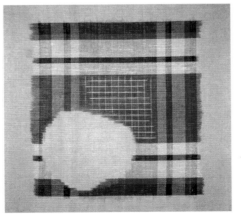

Virginia Davis, *Wholly Cloth,* 1990, double ikat on linen, 2/2 twill, one of a series of double ikats playing with the idea of tartans in Scottish culture, photo: Lee Fatheree.

Random sections of weft ikat woven together in a gestalt cloth, from Tenganon, Indonesia—an example of using extra or misdyed sections to create new projects.

Binding Clouds:
The Art of Central Asian Ikat

SUMRU BELGER KRODY

During the nineteenth century, the oasis towns of modern-day Uzbekistan were centers of high artistic innovation, most notably in the elegant art of creating ikat fabrics. These textiles epitomized the aesthetic ideals of both period and place. Even today, these brilliant textiles are appreciated for their remarkable visual impact and serve as inspiration for many leading fashion designers around the world (see photo, facing page).

The traditional term for the warp-ikat technique in Uzbekistan is *abrbandi,* which means "binding clouds." Binders for the ikat fabrics might have truly felt like they were trying to capture the clouds. They had to bind intricate designs to achieve the fine lines and details seen on these ikats while handling smooth, slippery, and unruly silk yarns. The exactness of the repeating motifs is an indication of technical control and collaboration between the designer and binder. The sophisticated color juxtapositions create striking designs.

Ikat was the dyer's art. The success of an ikat depended on the dyer's mastery of his craft and clear, unhindered communication with the designer. The dyer had to achieve a unified and beautiful design with vibrant, jewel-like colors through a succession of binding, dyeing, unbinding, and rebinding steps. Several weeks might be required to complete the dyeing process of a standard 210-yard ikat warp for a multicolored ikat fabric.

Ikat master Rosuljon Mirzaakhmedov in his ikat studio, Margilan, Uzbekistan, photo: Sumru Belger Krody.

Hanging or cover, Uzbekistan, Samarkand, or Bukhara, mid-19th century, silk, cotton, warp-faced plain weave, warp ikat, five loom-width panels sewn together, photo: The George Washington University Museum and The Textile Museum.

Hanging or cover cloth, Uzbekistan, Bukhara, first half 19th century, silk, cotton, warp-faced plain weave, warp ikat, four panels sewn together, photo: The George Washington University Museum and The Textile Museum.

The bold and imaginative designs on ikats were the creative work of *chizmakesh* or *abrbandchi* (designers). Using a small stick dipped in washable black dye or charcoal, they marked the outlines of the design onto the white warp yarns stretched on the patterning frame **(see a contemporary master on page 16)**. In order to produce fashionable fabrics each season, these designers needed to possess a thorough understanding of the ikat process, a good imagination and design sense, an ability to analyze old patterns, and a keen sense of the changing market. An experienced designer memorized designs and created new ones from memory. His younger apprentices might have used design aids to copy old motifs or think up new ones.

Artists and weavers always chose weave structures that gave prominence to the ikat-dyed warp yarns. The main weave structure favored was a warp-faced plain weave. In this structure, warp yarns were spaced densely on the loom so as to completely conceal the unpatterned weft yarns, and to emphasize the exquisite designs. In the finished fabric, the wrapped and unwrapped areas on the warp form designs and patterns of endless variety, from the dynamic and seemingly random to the precise and controlled.

Central Asian artists used nature as their design source, but they didn't attempt to reproduce the exact physical world in their art. Rather, they represented the mood or the spirit of nature. A clearly recognizable figure is a rare occurrence. Ikat artists stylized their designs by stripping the subject to its bare elements or concentrating on a single essence to represent the whole: the horns of a goat, the beak of a bird, the legs or tail of a scorpion, the silhouette of a tulip or a pomegranate. The tremendous variety and richness of the ikat designs seen on surviving hangings, covers, dresses, and robes are testimony to the designers' ambitious artistic goals, inventiveness, and improvisational skills **(see photo, facing page)**.

Ikat fabrics were considered precious and prestigious. They were expensive due to the high cost of silk and to a sophisticated production sequence that required a large and highly skilled workforce. Other factors affected the importance placed on textiles, especially luxury textiles such as ikat. Centuries of political turmoil and instability in Central Asia created an environment that forced people to accumulate and invest their wealth in portable items such as textiles and jewelry. They were light, made with expensive materials, required costly labor to produce, and didn't lose their value. Furthermore, it can be argued that wearing one's wealth was a lingering vestige of a nomadic past among long-settled societies.

It's impossible within the confines of a few pages or even a book to discuss thoroughly the fascinating and varied events that shaped the lives and attitudes of the people who designed, produced, and used the Central Asian ikat fabrics. We can only appreciate the preciousness of these ikats and the glorious time-honored civilization that produced them. We can also try to visually and intellectually reconnect Central Asian textile art to its original concept. The Central Asian ikat art is timeless, and understanding it provides the complex picture of shared culture among the designers, dyers, weavers, finishers, tailors, and consumers of these works of art.

Sumru Belger Krody is senior curator at the George Washington University Museum and The Textile Museum in Washington, DC, and editor-in-chief of The Textile Museum Journal. *Her research interest is late antique and Islamic textiles with a focus on the influences of textile techniques and structures on artistic, social, and economic power of textiles. She has worked in a curatorial capacity for many Textile Museum exhibitions and has authored and co-authored six books to accompany her exhibitions.*

CHAPTER TWO

equipment, materials & tools

We all know firsthand that using the right tool for a job can transform our experience. The physical laws that govern all equipment hold true with the tools we use in creating an ikat.

YARN-STRETCHING EQUIPMENT

All yarns to be used in making an ikat, whether warp or weft, are first measured and stretched under very even tension prior to the resist-wrapping process. Yarn stretching is handled quite simply in many parts of the world by pounding a stake into the ground to secure one end of the warp and another stake in the ground at a distance to secure the other end. The warp is then stretched under tension between the two stakes, ready to be wrapped.

The projects in this book use four different yarn-stretching systems: the warping board, loom raddles, ikat boards, and a DIY wooden frame. Try them all. Research pictures of systems from other countries (**see photo, facing page**). Improvise and adapt. Make your own version of stretching boards or a stretching frame. No method is more or less correct than the other, as long as it gets the job done and the end result is satisfactory.

WARPING BOARD: This is an excellent tool for ikat preparation that you already own or have access to and know how to use (**shown below left**). You'll stretch and wrap the first warp-ikat projects in this book using a warping board.

RADDLES: The loom raddle (**shown below right**) is another familiar weaving accessory that you may already own. It's used for keeping yarns organized and equally distributed when dressing the loom. Raddles look and function very much like ikat boards. They're a very good yarn-stretching and organizing tool when an ikat requires precisely following a pattern or a design plan. You'll need two raddles of the same size and four C-clamps to secure them to a table or flat work surface.

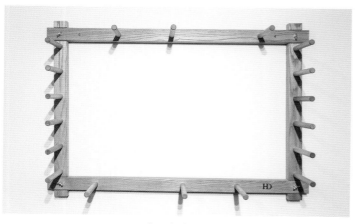

A warping board.

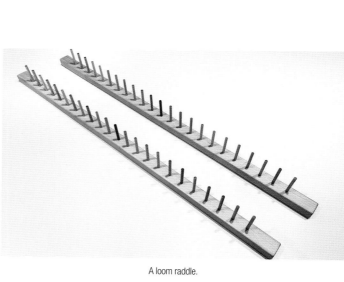

A loom raddle.

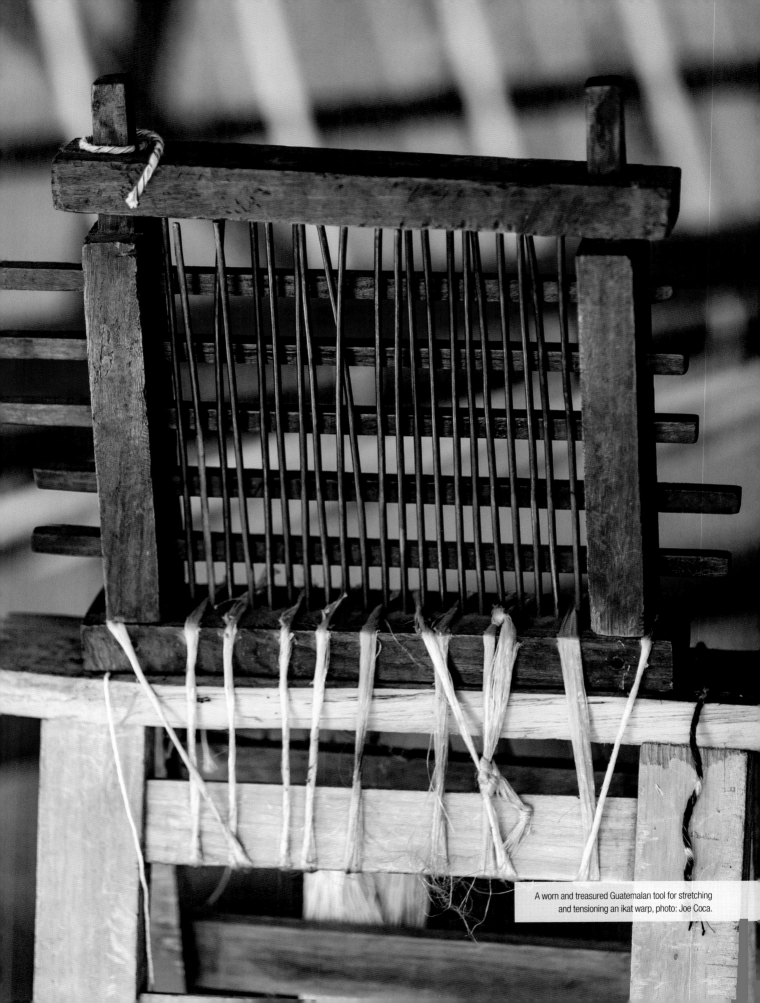

A worn and treasured Guatemalan tool for stretching and tensioning an ikat warp, photo: Joe Coca.

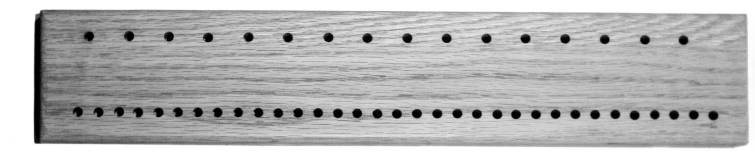

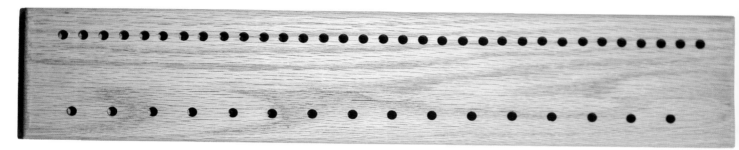

The matching components of a pair of ikat boards.

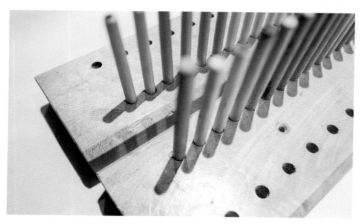

A pair of ikat boards assembled with removable wooden pegs.

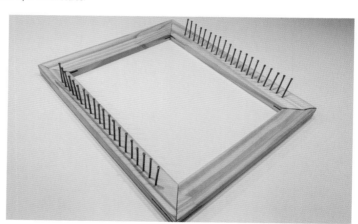

A DIY wooden stretching frame.

The Japanese cellophane tape the author uses as resist-wrap; it comes in different colors.

IKAT BOARDS: These are yarn-stretching boards, with evenly spaced holes precisely measured and drilled down the length of each board. A corresponding dowel or peg fits securely into each hole (**see photos, facing page**). Ikat boards resemble raddles, with the exception of removable wooden pegs rather than stationary nails. The advantage of the pegs is that they make yarn management a bit easier, allowing you to move them. The beauty of raddles and ikat boards is that they provide infinite flexibility in accommodating and tensioning any length of stretched yarn, from 5" (12.5 cm) to lengths of warp measuring 50' (15 m). They're the tools for the job if you're wrapping complex designs. Find instructions for making ikat boards in the Appendix, page 151.

DIY WOODEN STRETCHING FRAME: This is the yarn-stretching system I used for many years teaching weft-ikat workshops. These DIY ikat boards are made of wooden canvas stretcher frames from a craft/art supply store and finishing nails (**shown on facing page**). Find directions for making your own frame in the Appendix, page 149.

WRAPPING MATERIALS

Materials suitable for creating a resist-wrap must be impermeable to dye and flexible enough to wrap intricately and securely around fine threads. They have one job and one job only, and that is to cover and protect yarn from dye. Dental floss and raffia work as handy resists for small design areas. Plastic produce bags cut into strips make good resist-wraps for larger areas. When I first began experimenting with ikat, I cut up black garbage bags into strips of all sizes. A few years later I discovered commercial Japanese "ikat tape" and have been using this as my resist-wrapping material for over 30 years. This flexible cellophane-type tape (**shown on facing page**) splits easily into small strips and "clamps down" on fiber when placed in a hot dyebath. See Suppliers, page 154.

APPROACHES TO WARP-SHIFTING

The warp-ikat projects in this book explain how to use different warp-shifting methods and tools. The good news is that you don't *have* to buy or make anything to shift an ikat warp. You can get stunning results just by tugging on your warp threads and tying them at various lengths to the rear warp beam when warping your loom. There are cultures that have taken warp-shifting to the highest level of the art, creating fabrics that are the standard and signature by which we define ikat today.

STAGGERED KNOTS: When tying your warp ikat onto the back beam, divide a resist-dyed section into equal smaller sections and pull each section, staggering and adjusting the sections and shifting them to create a shape, such as an arrow, and then tie each group individually onto the back-beam rod (**shown below left**).

STAGGERED CORD TIES: Fasten a series of cords of different lengths in an uneven number sequence—3-5-7-9—onto your back-beam rod (**shown below right**). Then simply tie your small resist-dyed warp bundles to each section to create an automatic warp shift. Note that when beaming the warp, you'll have to comb through the shifted bundles and play with the tension to compensate for the pulled warp and to keep the tension even.

Staggered knots.

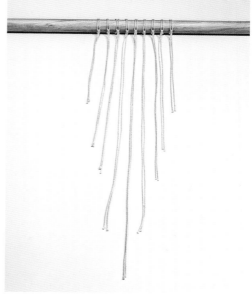

Staggered cord ties.

WARP-SHIFTING DEVICE: I found references to Japanese warp-shifting tools online and asked my local carpenter to make prototypes to use for projects in this book. These are tools that I hadn't previously used in my own ikat work; the result is a delightful discovery and adventure. The gadgets are fun, and the results are stunning. The warp-shifting device is a Japanese-inspired warp-shifter made of MDF or hardboard with staggered stairstep slits (**shown near left**). The smooth and well-sanded device is screwed onto a mounting board and clamped securely onto the back beam of the loom, creating an extended surface that influences the length of the ikat-warp threads. Warp sections are grouped and distributed within the slits. This is a fantastic tool to own if you're inspired to weave many versions of the same shifting pattern. Refer to the Appendix, page 152, for directions on making a simple warp-shifting tool.

DOWEL SHIFT: A thick dowel is added as an extension to the back warp-beam rod. Loop or tie several ikat-resisted warp sections to the dowel. Tie or loop the remaining warp sections onto the back-beam rod, as usual. This will automatically shift the warp groups (**see illustration below**).

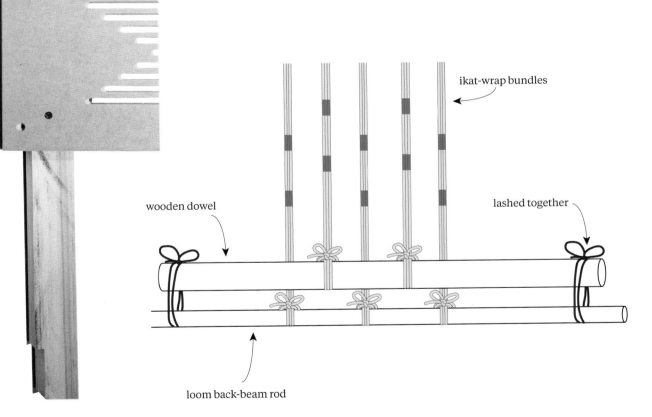

ikat-wrap bundles

wooden dowel

lashed together

loom back-beam rod

A warp-shifting device.

Dowel shift.

A Crocodile in the Cloth

WILLIAM INGRAM

In 1993 I was writing an article for an inflight magazine about the *geringsing* double-ikat textiles of Tenganan Pegeringsingan, in east Bali. While talking to Ni Wayan Sriani, a master weaver and dyer, I learned not to ask too many questions about the meanings of the traditional motifs in her textiles. She would give me names, but not meanings. When pressed, she said that sharing what she understood would not help me. I have spent many years since then trying to work out what she meant.

Geringsing means "against sickness" and marks a textile as protective in the unseen, animistic world of the spirits, both for an individual wearing it and the community using it in ceremony. A young Tengananese woman who wants to start making geringsing must make an offering at the Shiva temple on the steep, forested hill to the east of the village. This least ostentatious of shrines is just a small, square terrace with a dry-stone retaining wall. Weavers require a ceremony here, as their textiles are seen to intervene with life and death, which are the domain of Shiva.

While the markers of the weaver's intention to protect are not grand—a simple offering of the makings of the betel nut quid (a tobacco and powdered betel nut mixture) are tucked into one of the posts that holds the warp beam of the backstrap loom—it's the context that makes all the difference. The community maintains its complex textile tradition, its daily ritual practices, its strict architectural code, and its codified land management practices in order to embody an underlying worldview in all aspects of its material culture, including its textiles, its offerings, its buildings, and its landscape. This is learning by doing. People come to appreciate on a visceral level the intentions of the shared cosmology, the value system, and the ethics of

Left: Village entrance in Tenganan, Bali, legendary for its extraordinarily complex double-ikat cloth, photo: Threads of Life.
Right: Wrapping ikat on Prai Yawang and Rambu Eti's back porch in Tenganan Village, Bali, Indonesia, photo: Threads of Life.

their society by immersion within them. Intellectual understanding comes through decades of practice and is the mark of mastery—mastery that for the weaver concentrates all their experience into their textiles, making them protective. As Sriani pointed out, without any foundational experience, the meanings of the textiles and their motifs are unintelligible.

In the Malaka regency of Timor, Rosalia Bubu is one of the acknowledged masters of the local weaving tradition. Before she starts work on the ikat tying of a new cloth, she will both wait for a dream to tell her what motif to make, and make a betel nut offering in the clan house at the top of the village. The offering formally asks the ancestors for permission to make the cloth, though they are seen to have already spoken to her through the dream. A ritual presentation of the completed textile to the ancestors is also made in the clan house, again acknowledging their influence. While Bubu is a skilled dyer and weaver, it is her ritual experience—or rather the quality of her attention to the unseen world—that marks her as a master.

In the Dawan language that Bubu speaks, there's a word meaning both ancestor and crocodile that should only be spoken in ceremonial context. The saltwater crocodiles of the river estuaries around Timor can grow 17 feet (5.2 m) long and weigh a ton (1,000 kg). Regarded as ancestors, they are ritually fed during seasonal rites. During the ikat-tying process, once work on a crocodile motif is begun, Bubu must carry it to completion without a break. While she's including the crocodile in her cloth so that its power is available to the cloth's wearer, Bubu wants that power to be controlled and directed and wouldn't want to open the way for such a powerful figure to enter into her life without containing it properly. For her, the motif of the crocodile is not symbolic of a crocodile but it is an extension of crocodile-ness into the cloth **(see photo, page 30)**.

When we visit Tamu Rambu Hamu Eti in east Sumba, we often find her working on some aspect of textile production with the women of her household. Along the back porch of the traditional house where she lives, warp-ikat textiles can be found in the various stages of production. Often the warps of large men's hip-cloths, returned to their ikat frames after dyeing and prior to transfer to a backstrap loom, lean against the wall **(see page 28, right photo)**.

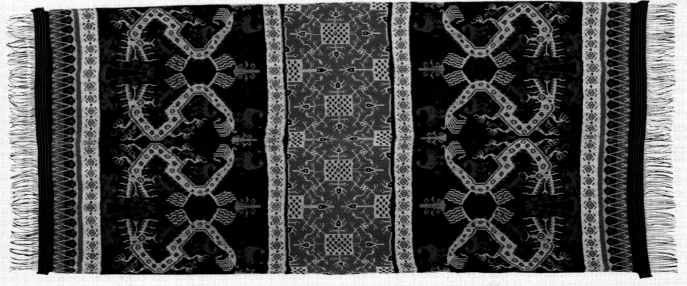

Geringsing double-ikat ceremonial cloth woven by Ni Wayan Sriani, 1998, photo: Threads of Life.

Double ikat by Rosalia Bubu, West Timor, Indonesia, photo: Threads of Life.

There's a comforting congruence between the textiles and the building (**see illustration below**). The ikat motifs on these cloths are arranged into seven fields. The center fields are identified with the roof apex of the traditional house, which is in turn identified with the realm of the primal ancestor. The fields on either side of the cloths' centers are equivalent to the loft space above the ceiling in the building's center, which is itself equivalent to the realm of divine ancestors. The motif fields outside these are identified with the floor area of the house and the abode of the living. The bands at the head and foot of the cloth are equivalent to the space under the house, amongst the pilings upon which the structure stands, an area which is itself identified with the realm of the dead who have not yet undergone the ceremonies to elevate them into the divine ancestry. For those interested in seeking them, further reciprocities can be found: the wooden pillars of the house bring the life of the forest into the building and maintain the living building as part of the forest, for example. The correspondences multiply and expand into the unseen fabric of the world, weaving the ikat textile into the house, the house into the village, the village into the watershed, the watershed into the island, and the people into the whole.

When we engage with these traditions, we're being invited to explore a direct and holistic way of participating in the world that's not easily, or perhaps not even possibly, expressed in language. Indeed, the inadequacy of any form of direct representation to intimate the animist experience leads to a form of communication dependent on knowledge embodied in the practices of everyday life and manifested through material culture, where deeper meanings are more potent than explicit significance. Of the surviving expressions of material culture to carry this wisdom, the most resilient and most ubiquitous in Indonesia are within the warp-ikat traditions of the textile arts.

William Ingram is co-founder of Threads of Life, a Bali-based social enterprise that has worked with over a thousand traditional weavers on twelve Indonesian islands since 1997 to improve livelihoods, support indigenous culture, and facilitate sustainable use of dye-plant resources. He has lived in Bali since 1993 and is the author of A Little Bit One O'clock: Living with a Balinese Family *and articles in academic publications, including* Textile Journal.

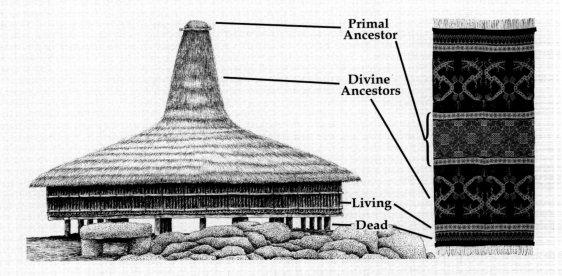

Illustration of the symbolic congruence between the design and structure of Indonesian textiles and the sacred village clan house, image: Threads of Life.

CHAPTER THREE | methods

I'm reminded each time I teach that there are many different ways to accomplish the same task. A case in point is that no two people in a workshop warp a loom in exactly the same manner. The same principle holds true for methods of preparing yarns to become ikat cloth.

WINDING WARP YARNS
FOR WRAPPING IKAT
ON THE WARPING BOARD

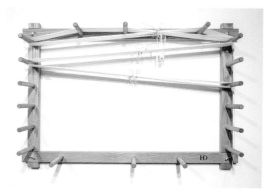

figure 1

The first two projects in this book, The Random Wrap Indigo Scarf and the Shifted-Warp Scarf, teach basic ikat yarn preparation: measuring a warp and resist-wrapping it while it's stretched on the warping board or reel (**figure 1**). One can wrap and encircle an entire hank of warp with one length of tape or isolate and measure smaller specific warp sections individually, counting threads, wrapping, and labeling them in separate groups on the warping board. In this case, all of the different sections are later gathered and collated in sequence, then loaded onto lease sticks, section by section, in preparation for dressing the loom (**figure 2**). Think of this as creating a palette of interchangeable warp-ikat design components.

figure 2

As your interest in and patience for ikat develops, you may want to tackle more elaborate designs than wrapping on the warping board allows. This method of wrapping yarns follows a design that is drawn as a wrapping pattern or guide, placed beneath your warp threads (**figure 3**). The Checkerboard Stole, page 102, teaches this next-level step, which involves removing a warp from the warping board and stretching it under tension on a tabletop.

USING A TWO-BOARD STRETCHING SYSTEM

Raddles and ikat boards are similar and totally interchangeable in appearance and function as pieces of ikat equipment. I refer to them interchangeably in this book. Both are excellent yarn-stretching and organizing tools for warp and weft ikat, used when an ikat design requires precisely following a wrapping pattern, also called a cartoon. To create this system, you'll need two boards of the same length and with even peg/nail spacing, and four 3" (7.5 cm) C-clamps. Clamp the boards opposite each other on a table. After the warp has been removed from the warping board, redistribute individual warp sections between the pegs and adjust the distance between the boards to create the desired yarn tension necessary for wrapping (**figure 4**).

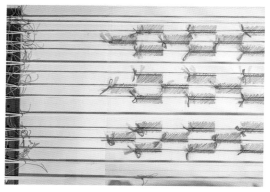

figure 3

figure 4

figure 5

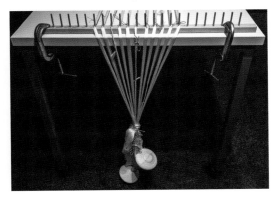

figure 6

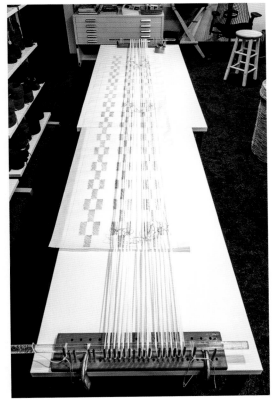

figure 7

What if your work surface isn't long enough to accommodate your warp? Try either one of these options:

▸ Use two tables or surfaces of the same height. Clamp one ikat board onto the end of one table and the other onto the end of the second table, opposite each other. Pull the tables apart to create the distance for the necessary warp tension. Insert a piece of foam core or matt board spanning the distance between the tables to create a continuous work surface (**figure 5**).

▸ If you have a long warp and a small table, clamp the ikat boards onto the ends of your worktable. Distribute and secure the warp at one end by looping the ends of the warp over the pegs or through a rod that is secured behind the pegs. Next, distribute the warp through the corresponding pegs of the second board. Allow the remaining warp length to hang off the ends of the table. Bundle the hanging warp and attach a 3–5 lb (1.4–2.3 kg) weight to provide the tension necessary for wrapping (**figure 6**). After you've wrapped the stretched warp sections on the table, advance the remaining unwrapped warp to the wrapping position on the tabletop, and hang and weight both ends. Do this in as many increments as it takes to completely wrap the warp.

Weavers are clever, and they've always stretched ikat warps longer than their table, room, or workshop can comfortably handle. Lack of space, equipment, materials, or time has never stopped mankind from dreaming big. In Uzbekistan, warps 230 yd (210 m) long were the standard. (For the record, that's ⅛ mile!) How does one resist-wrap such a long warp under tension? One technique is to layer and fold the warp over on itself, once, twice, or many times, picking up all of the threads of each layer and wrapping them together as one design unit. This explains the mirror-image repetition of patterns seen in many ikat fabrics. The layered stretching and wrapping of yarns is a well-practiced shortcut and time-saving tool worldwide.

USING A WRAPPING PATTERN/CARTOON

In tapestry weaving, the designs and drawn-to-scale images placed behind the warp threads to inform and guide the weaving process are called cartoons. In my studio, my assistants and I also refer to our ikat-wrapping patterns as cartoons. These drawings are an important design road map, indicating where to begin and end each area to be wrapped on every section of yarn, without making marks on the fibers themselves. A cartoon isn't necessary for a randomly wrapped warp, but it's very helpful for more detailed ikats.

To make a simple warp cartoon, cut a piece of paper the size of your desired finished piece. Then draw the pattern, indicating sections to be wrapped. Simply line up and tape the cartoon to the table between the boards of your yarn-stretching device, beneath the stretched yarns. Wrap the yarns above the marked sections (**figure 7**).

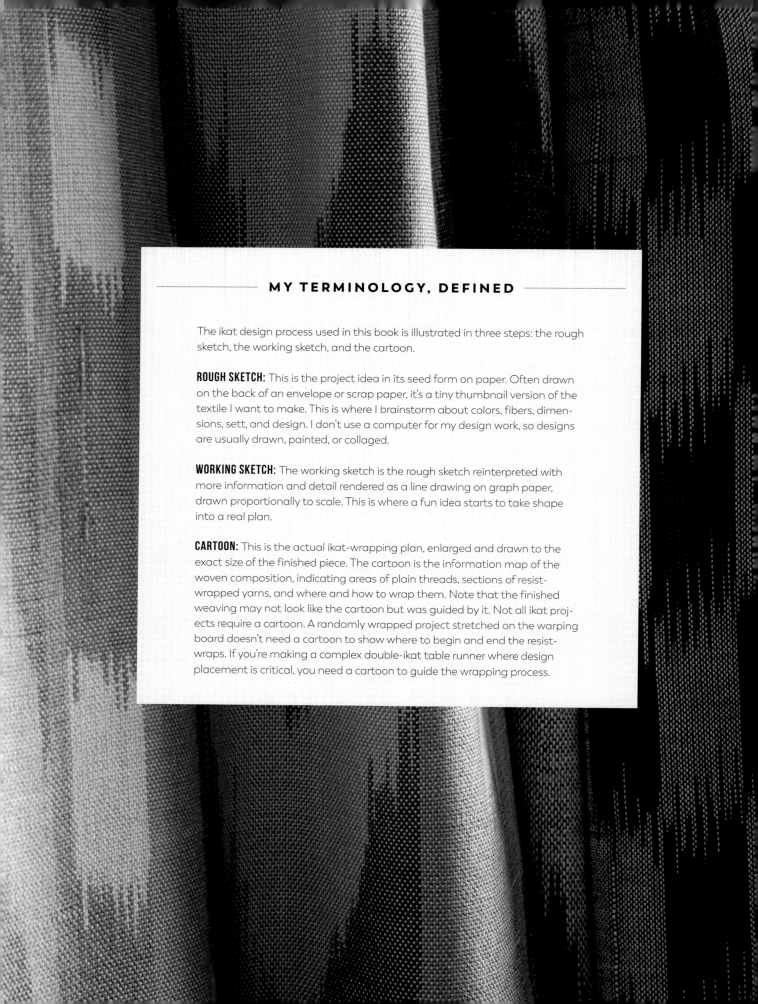

MY TERMINOLOGY, DEFINED

The ikat design process used in this book is illustrated in three steps: the rough sketch, the working sketch, and the cartoon.

ROUGH SKETCH: This is the project idea in its seed form on paper. Often drawn on the back of an envelope or scrap paper, it's a tiny thumbnail version of the textile I want to make. This is where I brainstorm about colors, fibers, dimensions, sett, and design. I don't use a computer for my design work, so designs are usually drawn, painted, or collaged.

WORKING SKETCH: The working sketch is the rough sketch reinterpreted with more information and detail rendered as a line drawing on graph paper, drawn proportionally to scale. This is where a fun idea starts to take shape into a real plan.

CARTOON: This is the actual ikat-wrapping plan, enlarged and drawn to the exact size of the finished piece. The cartoon is the information map of the woven composition, indicating areas of plain threads, sections of resist-wrapped yarns, and where and how to wrap them. Note that the finished weaving may not look like the cartoon but was guided by it. Not all ikat projects require a cartoon. A randomly wrapped project stretched on the warping board doesn't need a cartoon to show where to begin and end the resist-wraps. If you're making a complex double-ikat table runner where design placement is critical, you need a cartoon to guide the wrapping process.

WINDING WEFT YARNS
FOR IKAT WRAPPING

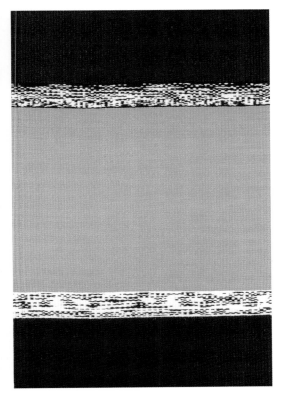

Mary Zicafoose, *San Jose* (detail), 2008, weft-faced ikat tapestry, wrapped, dyed, and woven wool on linen warp, collection of the Omaha Union for Contemporary Art, photo: Kirby Zicafoose.

Everything about weft ikat—the measuring, stretching, wrapping, and weaving—is "next-level" ikat. Weft ikat requires more advanced weaving skills and a different way of thinking. You need to consider the percentage of dyepot shrinkage of the resist-wrap weft and the degree that weft will beat in when woven, which will affect the number of woven picks per inch/cm. Both factors have a bearing on the accurate rendering of your design. Woven picks per inch/cm is calculated differently for each different type and weight of weft yarn.

Weft ikat requires that you learn to think like your weft yarn—no, actually, like *hundreds* of shots of weft yarns. Randomly wrapped and dyed wefts can become a busy colored mishmash and turn into visually bland and indistinct dashes and dots when *weft* yarns are carefully wrapped but then improperly calculated and carelessly woven. An exception is when sections of ikat-weft yarns are intentionally placed to create visually interesting patterning, as illustrated in the stripes of the tapestry shown near left, where the randomly woven shots of ikat yarns contrast with solid fields of color.

A rule of thumb when winding yarn for a controlled weft ikat is to first determine the desired woven width of the piece, and then space your stretching boards slightly wider than the desired width of your piece, to accommodate yarn shrinkage and arcing or bubbling your weft as you weave, approximately 3–5%. For example, if your desired woven width is 10" (25 cm), then your board will be set at a distance of approximately 10¼–10½" wider (26–27 cm), from peg to peg. Each full turn around the pegs represents two weft picks. Wind yarns evenly and firmly but at approximately the tension you would normally weave. If you pull the weft quite taut while stretching it between the boards, the yarns might actually weave in at a 9" (23 cm) width, and then you've lost the registration and accuracy of your design. The Seaside Placemat project, page 130, introduces beginning weft-ikat techniques.

TWINING, LABELING, AND ORGANIZING

After stretching the weft yarns, loosely twine the individual sections together at both ends (**figure 8**). This will keep your design area and yarn units sequentially organized. Don't twine too tightly or the twining material will form a resist on the fiber.

Label yarn sections while on the stretching board(s). Indicate the top and bottom, left and right, and/or section number (**figure 9**). Labels will assist you in laying out and collating your dyed unwrapped threads in order. They're equally important to maintain proper sequence in weaving in the weft. For this purpose, purchase water-resistant labels made of Tyvek, or create your own by recycling Tyvek envelopes, cutting them into strips, and punching holes in them. Write on the labels using a permanent laundry marker that doesn't bleed. When the twining and labeling is complete, sequentially thread the loops that go around the pegs onto a thicker piece of yarn—like pearls on a necklace, tied with a bow. This will assist in preventing tangling in the dyepot and help provide order when unwrapping and shuttling the dyed yarns.

figure 8

figure 9

Sheila Hicks (American, active in France, born 1934), *Mandarin Shrine,* 2016, linen, cotton, synthetic fibers, Joslyn Art Museum, Omaha, NE, museum purchase with funds from Joslyn Art Group, 2016, photo: Joslyn Art Museum.

RESIST-WRAPPING OF YARNS

Resist-wrapping yarn has only one purpose, and that is to create a resist or barrier on sections of fibers to protect them from taking on color in the dye-pot. Wrapping yarn for ikat is an art form in itself. Your first attempts may feel awkward. With practice, you'll develop a rhythm and a style, much like all of the repetitive tasks associated with weaving. Sections of wrapped fibers often take on their own sculptural quality and can be quite dramatic and beautiful. The American contemporary artist Sheila Hicks is famous for her wrapped sculptural installations that very much resemble massive hanks of ikat-wrapped threads (see photo on page 39).

Learn to resist-wrap yarns by starting with a small design section, as follows.

1. Begin by cutting a piece of resist-wrapping material approximately seven times longer than the area you'll wrap. In the example shown, the design area to be wrapped measures 3½" (9 cm) long, so I cut a piece of ikat-wrapping tape 25" (63.5 cm) long. Must you measure the tape each time you do an ikat wrap? Of course not. After a few wraps, you'll get a sense of how much tape you need to use to wrap an area. Too long a piece of wrapping material can split or double up on itself, much like what happens when you cut too long a piece of thread to sew on a button. But for the first wrap, do measure.

2. Place the tape on top of the hank of yarn, at the left end of your design, leaving a 2" (5 cm) tail of tape (figure 10).

3. Begin wrapping the tape around the yarns, holding the yarn firmly and overlapping the tape onto itself as you wrap to the right (figures 11 and 12). A firm tight wrap will create a clean sharp "line" and a high-contrast resist, which will discourage dye from wicking up under the ikat tape.

Should you want to encourage the dye to wick and bleed up under the tape, wrap loosely, particularly at the ends. This will result in a very blurry design edge, creating a mid-tone dye color.

4. When you reach the desired length of the area to be covered, pull the wrap securely (figure 13), returning in the direction you came. This overlapping will provide double coverage and extra resist security in the dyepot and allows both ends to reunite and be easily tied together, which you will do using the slipknot technique explained in the next paragraph.

figure 10

figure 11

figure 12

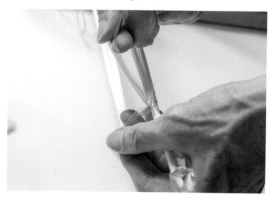

figure 13

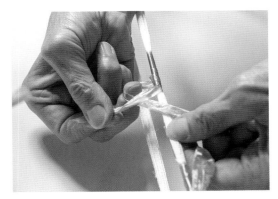

figure 14

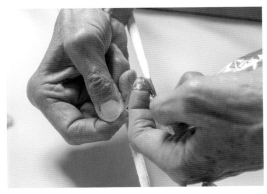

figure 15

figure 16

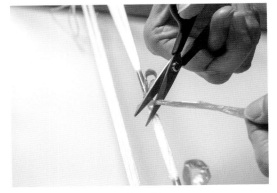

figure 17

Tie a slipknot as follows: Wrap the tape over your finger once, forming a loop (**figure 14**). Now push the tape through the loop (**figure 15**) and tighten the knot (**figure 16**). After dyeing, when it's time to remove the resist, the tape will unwrap and this knot will be very easy to untie with no cutting or scissors required. Simply pull out the loop, loosen the overall wrapping, and tug the starter tail. The slipknot tie takes some practice.

Do not secure the ends of the tape together using a double knot! It's a very tempting quick solution, but you'll then need scissors or a seam ripper to undo the knot when removing the ikat tape after dyeing, and you may inadvertently cut threads. Using a slipknot will make the untying process safer and so much faster.

5. After wrapping and knotting the resist areas, go back and double-check the wrapping accuracy. If a wrapped area turned out longer than desired, slide and compress the wrapping, shortening it. If it's not long enough, remove it and rewrap the area, or just add on more tape, overlapping the existing wrap. Also trim the tails to be approximately the same length (**figure 17**). This will eliminate long straggly tape ends from getting caught and wrapped around exposed yarn during dyeing.

WRAPPING LONG RESIST AREAS

Long wraps are managed by "adding on" ikat tape as you run out. Rather than tying a knot midway in a long section to be wrapped, overlap the short end of tape with a new long strip and continue wrapping. Secure your wrap as you go with a clothespin.

Note: Knots form compression and encourage dye wicking. Sometimes dye spots and splotches are not the desired result in a large area you're intending to protect from the dye. When adding on, always overlap the ikat tape for best results.

Hand-wrapped, dyed, and woven ikat yardage in the Guatemalan marketplace, photo: Joe Coca.

figure 18

WRAPPING MULTIPLE
SIMILAR RESIST AREAS

To expedite the wrapping process, sometimes similar pattern areas can be gathered and wrapped together. However, binding multiple sections in one big clump isn't always a foolproof method, as wrapping a big thick section of yarn encourages dye to wick up under the wrapping and sacrifices detail. For good results, first wrap 1 or 2" (2.5–5 cm) of each section according to the pattern and then gather and bundle the similar sections together, overlapping the wrap on the remaining yarn. The result will resemble fingers jutting out from a hand.

figure 19

WRAPPING LARGE AREAS: "BAGGING"

It's not always necessary nor actually very smart to hand-wrap every bit of long lengths of similar design areas. Over the years, I've developed this time-saving shortcut to make the resist-wrapping process more efficient and successful.

figure 20

Wrap the beginning of the long section(s) of yarn not to be dyed with ikat tape, then lift it off the board and place the remaining unwrapped yarn ends in a plastic freezer bag, rolling it firmly around the yarn hank (**figure 18**). Then tightly cover and bind the edges of the bag with ikat tape, as shown in **figures 19, 20,** and **21**.

figure 21

UNWRAPPING YARN

When the dyeing is complete, place the damp dyed yarns to be unwrapped on a dry towel to protect your work surface and clothing (**figure 22**). Then start unwrapping the resist ties.

figure 22

If you tied slipknots as described previously, simply pull the tail end (**figure 23**), loosen the wrap, and pull the wrapping off (**figure 24**). *Leave all identifying tags, labels, and twining on the yarn!* It's not yet time to remove any of this. You still need the information that the labels carry (**figure 25**).

If you tied very tight standard double knots—although you shouldn't have, because you should have tied slipknots, as described on page 41!—you'll need a pair of small sharp scissors and/or a seam ripper; very carefully cut off the end of the knot and remove the wrapping.

figure 23

Hang the dyed and now unwrapped sections of ikat yarn to air-dry. Note that if you use a hair dryer or the gentle cycle on your clothes dryer to accelerate drying a section of ikat-dyed yarn, you must then be consistent and dry all of the warp or weft for that project in the same manner. This is to equalize shrinkage. If one section of your ikat shrinks markedly more than the others, your design will be altered, particularly when using a fiber extremely prone to shrinkage, such as wool, in weft ikat. All fibers used in a project perform best when subjected to the same influences.

And what happens if the dyed, wrapped yarn dries before you have a chance to unwrap it? Nothing dramatic. The sections of dyed yarn will be dry and fulled, while the wrapped yarn will be damp and very compressed from the tight resist-wrapping. To make the yarn uniform, rinse the unwrapped hank of yarn, giving the different areas a chance to re-full themselves evenly, and then let dry.

figure 24

CAN YOU RECYCLE WRAPS?

Recycling wrapping materials is entirely personal preference. I don't reuse my ikat resist tape, but I do reuse large heavy-duty food bags over and over again to protect big areas of long multiple wraps.

figure 25

Indian Ikat— From Simple to Legendary

CHARLLOTTE KWON AND TIM MᶜLAUGHLIN

To this day artisans in India maintain several ikat traditions. Production varies from simple everyday cloths used as running fabric, shawls, saris, or *lunghis* (a man's wrap or sarong) to exquisite double silk ikat used ceremonially or exported to an international market.

The practice of ikat seems to confirm that there's something in the heart of the Indian crafts-person that delights in complexity. Techniques of tying and weaving are ingenious. Looms, boards for warp and weft preparation, starching brushes, bobbins, and spinning wheels are all made locally from simple materials. Everything can be easily modified. The presence of a clever hand in all of India's ikat is unmistakable.

The demands of ikat are several: a good geometric imagination; planning skills both in terms of pattern and process; and patience throughout the laborious tying, dyeing, untying, rety-ing, and dyeing stages—all of which must be completed before the actual weaving may begin. Such demands, however, are not always seen as tedious or oppressive; rather in many cases the complexity of the craft is a source of pride and the foundation of a cloth-based identity. This same pride fuels the evolution of more and more complex ikat as well as the regional variations in pattern that permit designs to be associated with particular districts and even villages, as described in the next pages.

Above left: Indian man wrapping a stretched cotton warp with strips of bicycle tires. Artists frequently use found and indigenous materials to create resist-wraps, photo: Maiwa School of Textiles, Tim McLaughlin. Above right: A master weaving an intricate double-ikat pattern, photo: Maiwa School of Textiles, Tim McLaughlin.

Double ikat woven patola, photo: Maiwa School of Textiles, Tim McLaughlin.

TELANGANA

South of the sprawling metropolis of Hyderabad, in south central India, in the state of Telangana, ikat traditions are geometric, simple, and deftly executed. Patterns are generally worked across the entire field of cloth. Single ikats may be worked on either warp or weft threads and although cotton is the preferred fiber, silk is also used. Double ikats are made, often with two weavers sitting side by side on a pit loom. The first weaver throws the shuttle and works the heddles with foot levers, while the second weaver attends to the registration of the pattern through the fine adjustment of weft threads after each throw of the shuttle. Warps are stretched and starched in a lane or village street, but they're resist-tied inside, where the artisans can work in the shade. For tying, old bicycle inner tubes are cut into strips about a quarter-inch wide. These provide an excellent resist, are in seemingly endless supply, and can be quickly tied and removed.

ODISHA

The geography of the state of Odisha (previously Orissa), with its hills and forests, has led to the evolution of regionally distinct ikat styles. The best known of these is the Sambalpur sari. The term denotes not a single garment but a constellation of patterns named for places such as Sonepur, Bijapur, Nuapatna, and Barpali. These weaves were made for local consumption and for wider export from the textile markets of Sambalpur. Locals can still identify a woman's village through pattern recognition: a sari can be more specific than a regional accent. Odisha ikat is worked on cotton, bombyx silk, and wild tussar silk. Designs include geometric motifs, figurative work inspired by sculptural elements of the Jagarnath temples, scripts, and folk designs based on Warli motifs from Maharashtra. Thread is used for the resist tying. Young artisans can tie groups of weft threads with bewildering quickness. In villages, weft boards are the weaver's laptop, carried from place to place and worked on throughout the day. Both men and women tie the threads. Weft preparation is often completed in small groups on a veranda or in the shade of trees. The omnipresence of the weft boards in the community attests to the fact that everyone knows the art.

Artist with his portable ikat board, India, photo: Maiwa School of Textiles, Tim McLaughlin.

PATAN PATOLA

For thousands of years the elaborate double ikats known as patolas have been made by the Salvi community of northwestern India. Patola is a holy silk cloth. It's believed that by wearing patolas containing religious and miraculous powers, one feels God. Today the last surviving family of patola weavers lives in Patan—hence the alliterative moniker Patan patola. These elaborate prestige items were made for an international textile trade (they're still heirlooms in Indonesia and many parts of Southeast Asia). The multiple colors are achieved through the use of natural dyes on fine silk threads and require months of tying and dyeing before weaving may begin.

Motifs and layout of patterns on the cloth are chosen from a traditional set. Clientele from Muslim, Hindu, and Jain communities all have a favored repertoire of designs. Weaving is done on a loom with suspended heddles that permit the weaver to tilt the frame to catch the light in order to check registration. Weaving is extremely slow as the artisan will trace each thread and make fine adjustments along the length of the cloth. The weaver uses a pencil-length steel needle to track and separate threads while working. The tightness of the weave, exactness of the registration, complexity of the design, and number of colors are the criteria by which these masterpieces are judged.

Charllotte Kwon is the owner and founder of Maiwa and the Maiwa School of Textiles, Vancouver, BC, Canada. Tim McLaughlin is a writer and photographer. Together, the two work to promote the continuation of traditional textile techniques through research, publications, documentaries, and lectures.

Bolts of beautiful Indian hand-wrapped, dyed, and woven ikat cloth, photo: Maiwa School of Textiles, Tim McLaughlin.

CHAPTER FOUR | dyeing

Ikat is a weaving process that entirely depends upon dyeing for its success. Traditionally each separate task in the ikat process was extremely specialized and managed by one highly trained craftsman or shop. Today being an ikat weaver means you're also an ikat dyer. In this context, what happens in the dyepot is actually more critical than what happens at the loom.

No steps in the ikat process can be skipped or mechanized, and certainly not the dyeing. The projects in this book don't use commercial variegated yarns, space dyeing, or painted warps. The woven effects of these types of surface-dyed fibers may share some visual similarities, but they're simply not resist-wrapped ikat. The serendipitous alchemy of wrapped fibers resisting, absorbing, and wicking color in a dyepot is what makes each ikat unique. In many worlds, past and present, the term ikat is synonymous with one-of-a-kind textiles.

There's quite an assortment of dye products and systems, both synthetic and natural, available to the weaver. I encourage you to use the systems you're familiar with, but also to experiment with and expand on what you don't know. The information and directions I provide may be different from the way you've been taught. Tweak and adapt the ikat projects and the dye recipes to reflect your experience level and personal taste.

Don't forget to write down everything that you do. Tomorrow you won't remember which section or how many times the resist-wrapped yarn hanks were dipped into the indigo vat, or how or why you tweaked a dye recipe. Good record-keeping is a learned habit. For repeatable results, you must develop a system of organizing your notes.

DYE SAFETY

This book provides instruction in basic dyeing. Step-by-step directions are included in how to build, dye, and maintain an indigo vat and how to dye with fiber reactive dyes. Whether you're a new dyer or a veteran to creating color, I must emphasize caution in use of all dye materials and the habit of safe procedures.

▸ Give some thought to where to best create a dye space. You don't need much real estate. Work outside or in a well-ventilated area of your garage or basement, but *not* in your kitchen, even if you have a great oven hood above your range. You don't want to contaminate your food-preparation area!

▸ Read through all steps of the dye instructions before you get started, even if you're experienced, and especially if it's been a while since you last dyed. Knowledge is power.

▸ Invest in the right tools for the job: glass, enamel or stainless steel pots, graduated cylinders, measuring tools, a reliable heat source, and a worktable.

▸ Purchase a gram scale. They're inexpensive and will allow you to weigh with accuracy.

▸ Gather up and clean your tools and supplies and lay them out in order of use. *Do not* use your kitchen utensils. If you do, they should then permanently join your cadre of dye-studio equipment; they're no longer safe to use with food.

▸ When handling dyes and mordants, always wear rubber gloves, your "project" clothing, and a protective apron. I use long Sol-Vex gloves produced by Ansell.

▸ Wear a dust mask or respirator when you're using dyes, auxiliaries, and mordants in their powdered form. These substances are most dangerous as powders, and are easily airborne, irritating eyes and nasal passages. I mix all powders outdoors. Fine airborne dye powders can end up endlessly circulating through your home HVAC system.

▸ Never bring food into the dye area, and do not eat while dyeing.

Safety first!

DYEING WITH INDIGO

It should come as no surprise that plants are the most important sources of dyes traditionally used in the resist processes. Historically, the harvesting, recipes, and specific processes of dye plants were often jealously guarded secrets of a family, workshop, or village. In Indonesia the dyeing of ikat is an art that's still carefully upheld today as spiritual ritual and sacred practice. This intense pride, exclusive ownership, and the almost supernatural significance of dye processes contributes to the mystique surrounding many dye colors and types of cloth.

Falling into this exotic and almost mystical category is indigo, among the oldest and most important of dye plants. With a history dating more than 3,000 years, nearly every global ikat tradition employs indigo. It's the dye of choice in regions of Japan and Asia where yarn and fabric are traditionally and purposefully only dyed one color.

I've spent three decades avoiding indigo. I wasn't indifferent to it, just actually a bit afraid of the legendary plant. I understand any reluctance you might have when I suggest that you concoct an indigo vat in a plastic garbage can in your garage, keeping it warm with an electric blanket and feeding it with sugar as regularly as you feed your dog. I understand your reservation. But, please, do it anyway. Absolutely nothing compares to ikat dyed in indigo. There's something etheric, elemental, and extremely satisfying in this process. Ikat and indigo, are, after all, ancient partners.

MAKING A 1-2-3 INDIGO VAT

The indigo-dye system I use originated from the recipe by Michel Garcia, the French botanist and natural dyer.

The name "1-2-3 Indigo Vat" refers to the proportions of the three ingredients used to build the vat: one part indigo pigment to two parts pickling lime to three parts fructose. It's an easy recipe to remember.

Indigo comes from fresh leaves. Sometimes the leaves are dried or composted, but they are most commonly available as a powdered pigment. When combined in water with an alkaline (calcium hydroxide) and a reduction material (fructose), the indigo pigment becomes soluble in the vat through a process called reduction. Reduction converts the indigo to a soluble form. Without this reduction, the indigo pigment is not soluble in the water and will not dye.

I built an indigo vat using this recipe one year ago and have been dyeing in the vat regularly since. Every indigo project in this book was dyed using this same well-fed vat, set up in a trash can that I keep in my backyard in the summer and move to my basement for the winter. I've been wrapping and dyeing ikat yarns for almost four decades but dyeing in an indigo vat for only a small fraction of that time. It's never too late to change, to learn, to take a risk, to try something new.

pH strips, powdered indigo, pickling lime, fructose, and a plastic container containing small stones are essential for creating a 1-2-3 indigo vat.

Set up your vat in a large trash can.
Placing it on a dolly allows you to move it easily.

RECIPE FOR A 1-2-3 INDIGO VAT

This will make a vat large enough to dye many indigo-dyed projects, and if maintained, can last for weeks or months. Before beginning, read all the instructions to familiarize yourself with the process.

Remember to wear gloves, an apron, and a dust mask or respirator when weighing dyes and pickling lime! The small particles can become airborne and may be irritating.

PROCEDURE

1. Heat water to just below boiling, 160–180°F (71–82°C), then pour the hot water into the plastic jar until it is about half to three-quarters full.

2. In this step, you'll prepare the indigo pigment by crushing and hydrating the powder. To accomplish this, put on your rubber gloves and apron, then place the measured indigo powder in the plastic jar along with a few marbles or stones, which will assist with agitation. Add enough warm water to wet all the powder, place the lid on the jar tightly, and shake vigorously for a few minutes to hydrate the powder (**figure 1**). The hydration makes it easier for the indigo to go into reduction and become soluble (**figure 2**).

3. Add the liquid-crushed indigo to the vat, pouring it through a strainer to capture the marbles (**figures 3 and 4**). Rinse the container and marbles well in the vat so all of the indigo goes into the mixture (**figure 5**).

4. Dissolve the measured fructose sugar in 2 c (0.5 l) of boiling water, then add it to the vat.

5. Put on your protective mask, then dissolve the measured pickling lime in 2 c (0.5 l) of cold water. Add it to the vat (**figure 6**).

6. Your vessel should be nearly full of warm indigo/sugar/lime solution. If not, add more hot water to reach the full level of 5 gallons (18 l). Dip your pH indicator paper into the vat to check the alkalinity (**figure 7**). If the three ingredients have been used in the correct proportion, the pH will be approximately 12–13. (See page 60 for information on maintaining the correct pH.) Stir the vat carefully by placing the dowel rod in the center of the vat, and make a circular movement, creating a vortex in the vat. This will incorporate any solid material at the bottom of the vessel and minimize the introduction of oxygen. Wait approximately 30 minutes and stir again. Cover the vat and allow to sit for several hours or overnight for full reduction before the first dyeing.

7. The vat is ready for use when a coppery skim with a few dark blue bubbles appears on the surface and the liquid below the surface begins to turn yellow/green and clear (**figure 8**). Dip a test piece of yarn into the vat for a few seconds. If it comes out yellow-green and then turns blue when exposed to the air, the indigo is reduced, and the vat is ready for dyeing. If the yarn does not come out of the vat yellow/green, allow the vat more time to reduce.

SUPPLIES

5 gal (18 l) water
300 g fructose (fruit sugar)
100 g indigo powder
200 g pickling lime (calcium hydroxide)

EQUIPMENT

pot for heating water
hotplate or burner
thermometer
plastic jar with tight-fitting lid
5-gal (18-l) plastic container for the vat
  (This dye vessel should be taller than
  it is wide and have a lid.)
long rubber gloves
apron
a few marbles or stones
strainer
heat-resistant measuring cup
dust mask or respirator
pH paper
long dowel for stirring

figure 1

figure 2

figure 3

figure 4

figure 5

figure 6

figure 7

figure 8

DYE PROCESS FOR A 1-2-3 INDIGO VAT

Hot water was used to start the quick reduction vat described on page 56, but once the indigo has been reduced, all fibers are dyed at ambient room temperature. Dyeing resist-wrapped sections of yarn is accomplished much like dyeing regular skeins of yarn. Beforehand, you'll need to scour the sections (see bottom of page 60) and pre-wet them. Before you start, read all the instructions to familiarize yourself with the process.

PROCEDURE

1. Place the mesh laundry bag carefully into the dye vat and drape the top of the bag over the sides of the vat, adjusting the length so it doesn't touch the bottom of the vat or slide back in (**figures 9 and 10**). Secure the top with a cord or large rubber band. The net will keep your yarns from touching the bottom of the bucket during dyeing. Excess lime, indigo, and sugars settle at the bottom of the vat as sediment while the reduced indigo, a clear yellow liquid, is at the top. If the yarns settle in the bottom, they won't dye properly.

2. Set the container of cold water beside the vat. Wearing long rubber gloves, carefully immerse the scoured, pre-wetted yarns into the indigo vat, keeping the yarns completely submerged in the liquid (**figure 11**). Indigo only dyes fibers it comes in direct contact with, so gently open and work dye into the yarns with your fingers so all the fiber is exposed to the dye. All movements within the vat should be very gentle to minimize the introduction of oxygen. Move yarns smoothly along the sides of the vat; do not agitate up and down.

3. Leave the yarns in the vat for 10–20 minutes in order for the indigo to penetrate the fibers. Then, gently squeeze the fiber out while it's still underneath the surface of the vat.

SUPPLIES

vat of reduced indigo dye

EQUIPMENT

mesh laundry bag that fits over the top of the bucket/vat
cord or large rubber band
long rubber gloves
container of cold water

figure 9

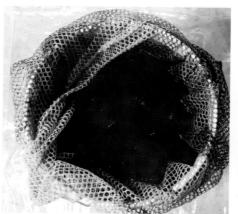

figure 10

figure 11

4. Carefully remove the yarns from the vat. They will be yellow-green in color and begin to turn blue as they are exposed to the air and start to oxidize (**figure 12**). Immediately plunge yarns into the container of cold water. This continues the oxidation and removes any dye that hasn't attached to the yarns (**figure 13**). Hang to dry, separating and exposing the areas of yarn that aren't resist-wrapped to the air.

Saturated deep blues are obtained by multiple dips, not multiple hours submerged in the vat. Once the yarn is fully oxidized, it can be dyed again to achieve deeper color. Allow at least 30 minutes for full oxidation before returning yarns to the vat for further dyeing.

NEUTRALIZING THE YARNS

Your yarn is now beautifully dyed, but you aren't done yet! The final important step is to neutralize the indigo-dyed yarn. When you've achieved the desired shade of blue, neutralize the alkaline lime in the yarns by soaking them for at least 20 minutes in a room-temperature solution of ½ c (125 ml) white vinegar in 1 gallon (4 l) water. Remove the yarns and rinse well in tap water. Then, for cotton yarns, simmer for 10 minutes in a pot of water with a drop or two of Synthrapol. There's no need to simmer wool and silk yarns, but soak them for 10 minutes in very hot tap water with Synthrapol. Let the yarns cool, then rinse until clear.

DRYING THE YARNS

After dyeing is complete, squeeze out as much of the excess water as you can before unwrapping the ikat. You can do this by hand, in the gentle spin cycle of your washing machine, or by using a portable tabletop mini laundry spinner. Tabletop spinners are terrific because they cut down on yarn drying time. See The Laundry Alternative in the Resources section. Once dyeing is complete, it's best to let the yarns dry overnight.

figure 12

figure 13

MAINTAINING THE pH OF THE INDIGO VAT

The alchemy of indigo, pH, and reduction must be kept in balance for the magic of indigo to happen. Each time you dye, no matter how careful you are, this balance is naturally disturbed with oxygen entering the vat and the pH slightly shifting. This is simply part of the process, requiring that the dyebath be properly maintained. Signs of a weary vat are blue water instead of green, murky water instead of clear, and yarn appearing blue, not yellow-green, when leaving the vat.

> ▸ Feed the vat approximately 1–2 tablespoons of fructose sugar after every dyeing session. Gently stir to bring up the sediment from the bottom of the vat. Then stir it gently in one direction, to minimize the introduction of oxygen. Allow the vat to rest at least 3–4 hours. As soon as the liquid is clear yellow again, the vat is ready for dyeing.

> ▸ Monitor the pH and add more lime if the pH goes below 10. Start with a sprinkle or two and check the pH after each addition until the pH has risen. When the vat starts producing only a very light blue color, despite having an accurate pH, then more sugar may be needed. It is also possible that the indigo may be exhausted. This is an indication that it's time to refresh all ingredients, including indigo (one tablespoon at a time), or build a fresh new vat. This indigo vat can be maintained for many days, weeks, and months.

DYEING CELLULOSE VS. PROTEIN FIBERS

When the vat is newly made, the pH will be very high. Although it's suitable for dyeing cellulose fibers right away, the high alkalinity can damage wool or silk yarns. After about two weeks, the quick reduction vat begins to ferment, and the pH starts to go down. At this point protein fibers can be dyed safely in the vat. Plan ahead if you intend to dye wool or silk.

A NOTE ON SCOURING

Scouring or prewashing yarns is a critical step in preparation for dyeing. Don't skip it to save time. Most fibers contain naturally occurring coatings; if you don't remove them, dye will attach to the coating and not the yarn. Over time, when the coating breaks down, so does the color. Scouring also removes any natural oils or commercial residue from the manufacturing process that might inhibit or block the color from uniformly adhering to the yarns. It opens up the fiber so it will more agreeably drink up color. Dyeing is a process of courtship and wooing—convincing yarn to accept color and color to jump onto yarn. Think of scouring as the first date, step one of laying the foundation for a lifelong, vibrant partnership. Scour all cellulose yarns in a stainless steel pot by boiling them for a minimum of 10 minutes in a small amount of Synthrapol or dish soap and a pinch of soda ash. Unmercerized yarns may need a longer or additional scour. Don't boil silk or wool; instead, soak in hot water and Synthrapol for 20–60 minutes.

USING SYNTHETIC DYES

Just as certain wines are best paired with certain foods, bringing out the best in each other, certain fibers are elementally more compatibly paired with certain dyes. The right fiber/dye pairing is the difference between dye particles lying on top of a strand of yarn, and washing or "crocking" off, as opposed to the dye molecules actually bonding with the yarn, forming a covalent bond with the protein or cellulose molecule. An incompatible yarn-dye process can also damage and shorten the life of the fiber.

Cotton, rayon, Tencel, bamboo, linen, jute, hemp, ramie—all yarns made from plant fibers—are very successfully dyed using a family of cold-water alkaline dyes called fiber reactive dyes. Silk can also be dyed in the same way. Procion MX and Cibacron F are brand names of standard fiber reactive dyes, available through many online sources and at fabric stores and craft shops. This family of dyes is easy to use and has excellent wash- and lightfastness, yielding bright, clear colors. The downside is these dyes require a lot of rinsing, resulting in some dye waste. Note that the liquid in your dyepot will not be exhausted and clear at the end of the dye session.

Wool, alpaca, mohair, angora, cashmere, and silk—yarns from animal or protein fibers—are sensitive to high pH and like to be dyed in hot-water acidic dyes. Protein fibers drink up and molecularly bond with dye color best when accompanied by auxiliary agents like acid (vinegar, citric acid crystals) and salt. Acid dyes produce vivid colors with very good lightfastness and are very easy to use. When the dye/fiber ratio is correctly balanced, the dyebath will be clear at the end of the dye session, with all color having jumped onto the yarn.

This book provides instruction in only one synthetic dye system, fiber reactive dyes. Most of the projects involve cotton, linen, and Tencel, which are cellulose fibers, with silk being an exception to the rule. Silk is a chemical chameleon, responding well to both fiber reactive and acid dye systems. For the sake of simplicity of instruction, I've also included a recipe for adapting cold-water fiber reactive dyes to dye protein fibers in an acidic hot-water immersion procedure. Using this method, both families of fibers can be dyed with fiber reactive dyes, using one convenient and simple synthetic dyeing system.

CALCULATING WEIGHT OF FIBER

Unlike indigo, when dyeing with fiber reactive dyes, you need to calculate the weight of fiber (WOF) in order to determine the amount of dye that is needed. When dyeing bundles of wrapped ikat fibers, you must take into account that your dry WOF number is not an accurate calculation for dyeing; a percentage of the yarn is covered with a resist-wrap and is not going to be exposed to dye. When calculating dry WOF before dyeing, first estimate the approximate area that will actually be dyed (areas that are *not* wrapped).

For example: Let's say the total dry weight of the wrapped ikat section is 12 oz (340 g). You guesstimate that approximately 60 percent of the yarn will be dyed.

To calculate your WOF of the surface area to be dyed, multiply the total weight by the guesstimated percentage that is not wrapped.

STANDARD MEASURE: 12 oz total fiber weight × 0.60 = 7.2 oz to be dyed
METRIC: 340 g total fiber weight × 0.60 = 204 g to be dyed

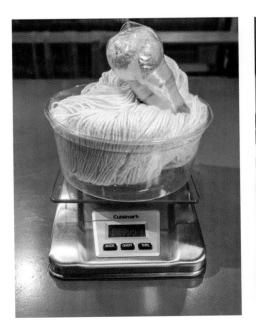

DYEING CELLULOSE FIBERS (AND SILK) WITH FIBER REACTIVE DYES

Before you begin, read all the instructions to familiarize yourself with the various steps of the process.

PROCEDURE

1. Weigh the dry fiber and estimate the amount of fiber to be dyed. Tie hanks or skeins of yarn loosely in several spots to avoid excessive tangling in the dyepot. (Take into account that the modus operandi of yarn is to get completely tangled in a dyepot.)

2. Pre-wet and scour the cellulose yarns (see page 60).

Rinse well.

3. Refer to the chart on the facing page to determine the quantity of dye to use, then weigh (or measure) the desired amount of dye powder.

Continued on page 66

SUPPLIES

water

Synthrapol or a mild dish soap such as Dawn or Ecover

soda ash (sodium carbonate)

Procion MX or Cibacron F fiber reactive dye powders

table salt, noniodized

Metaphos (an optional water softener)

vinegar (if dyeing silk)

EQUIPMENT

gram scale or measuring cups and spoons

stainless-steel pot for scouring and boiling out

hotplate or burner

small nonreactive (plastic, glass, or stainless steel) container

thermometer

large nonreactive container for dyebath

stirring rod

long rubber gloves

QUANTITIES FOR IMMERSION DYEING OF CELLULOSE WITH FIBER REACTIVE DYES

When calculating dye and chemical quantities, you'll achieve the most accurate results by using metric measurements, a gram scale, and graduated cylinders, making the metric system the preferred method for dyeing.

All quantities for dyes and chemicals are based on the WOF.

METRIC

Desired Shade	Light Value	Medium Value	Dark Value
Water	WOF × 20	WOF × 20	WOF × 20
Dye powder	WOF × 0.5%	WOF × 2%	WOF × 4%
Table salt	WOF × 50%	WOF × 50%	WOF × 100%
Soda ash	WOF × 10%	WOF × 10%	WOF × 10%

STANDARD MEASURE

You may use standard measurements as an alternative to metric measurements. Quantities given are to dye 1 pound of fiber.

Desired Shade	Light Value	Medium Value	Dark Value
Water	2½ gal	2½ gal	2½ gal
Dye powder	1 tsp	1 tbs	2 tbs
Table salt	1 cup	1½ cups	2 cups
Soda ash	5 tbs	5 tbs	5 tbs

Place the dye in a small nonreactive container and dissolve it in a small amount of tepid water (**figure 14**). Set aside. Place water (again referring to the chart on page 65 to determine how much you need) into the large nonreactive container and heat it to 100–150°F (38–66°C). Add the dissolved dye to it and stir.

4. Add the scoured and rinsed yarn, stirring for 5 minutes. Wearing gloves, stir or hand-manipulate your resist-wrapped yarns attentively while they're in the dyepot. Pay attention to areas where the ties are very close to each other, with little exposed yarn surface between ties. Massage and "open up" these areas with your fingers, encouraging the dye to enter and penetrate into the fibers. *Never assume that because the yarn is resist-wrapped and finally into the dye-pot that you're now home free.*

TIP: If you have just one section or a complex web of resist-wrapped fibers that you don't want submerged in the scour or dyebath, you must get clever and create a support system—using ikat tape, clothespins, or whatever you can think of—to successfully keep sensitive wrapped areas above and out of the liquid in the dyepot (**figure 15**).

5. Referring to the chart on page 65 for the proper amounts, weigh and dissolve the measured salt and a few grams of Metaphos (an optional water softener if your water is hard) in a container of hot water. Remove the yarn from the dye-bath and add the salt solution to the dyebath. Return the yarn to the bath and stir continuously for 10–15 minutes.

6. Referring to the same chart for the correct amount, measure the soda ash and completely dissolve it in warm water (**figure 16**). Remove the yarns from the dyebath and stir the dissolved soda into the bath. Return the yarns to the dyebath (**figure 17**). Stir frequently for 5 minutes and then occasionally for the next 60 minutes.

7. After an hour, dyeing is complete. Remove the yarns from the dyebath. Rinse the yarn thoroughly (**figure 18**). Add fresh water and a drop or two of Synthrapol to your stainless-steel pot (**figure 19**). Add the yarn and boil out the excess dye for 5–10 minutes. Rinse until clear. Discard the dyebath. ***Note:*** When dyeing silk, rinse the fiber carefully in this step, but do not boil it. Neutralize the alkaline dye in the silk fiber by soaking the yarn for 10 minutes in a vinegar bath of ¾ c (177 ml) vinegar to 1 gal (3.75 l) of water per pound (454 g) of fiber.

figure 14

figure 15

figure 16

figure 17

figure 18

figure 19

DYEING PROTEIN FIBERS WITH FIBER REACTIVE DYES

Protein fibers require a different version of alchemy and wooing to convince these yarns to open up and accept permanent color. Fiber reactive dyes can successfully be used to dye protein fibers, as long as they're used with the proper auxiliary chemicals, Glauber's salt, and a form of nontoxic acid such as household white vinegar.

PROCEDURE

1. Wet and scour the fiber by soaking it in a warm Synthrapol bath for at least 1 hour. Rinse.

2. Refer to the chart below for percentages of supplies to use. Weigh out the water, dye, and all auxiliary chemicals and add them to the dyepot. Stir well.

3. Add the yarn and bring the temperature up slowly to 200°F (93°C). Hold at temperature for 40 minutes, stirring frequently. Turn off the heat, leaving the yarns in the pot while the dyebath cools. Then rinse the yarns thoroughly.

After dyeing is complete, squeeze out as much of the excess water as you can before unwrapping the ikat. You can do this by hand, in the gentle spin cycle of your washing machine, or by using a portable tabletop mini laundry spinner. Tabletop spinners are terrific because they cut down on yarn drying time.

SUPPLIES

water

Synthrapol or a mild dish soap such as Dawn or Ecover

fiber reactive dye powders

Glauber's salt (sodium sulfate)

white vinegar

EQUIPMENT

nonreactive (plastic or stainless steel) container for wetting the fiber

gram scale or measuring spoons

stainless-steel pot for the dyebath

stirring rod

hotplate or burner

thermometer

gloves

QUANTITIES FOR IMMERSION DYEING OF PROTEIN WITH FIBER REACTIVE DYES

Desired Shade	Light Value	Medium Value	Dark Value
Water	WOF × 40	WOF × 40	WOF × 40
Dye powder	WOF × 0.25%	WOF × 1%	WOF × 3%
Glauber's salt	WOF × 3%	WOF × 3%	WOF × 3%
White vinegar	WOF × 12%	WOF × 12%	WOF × 12%

STANDARD MEASURE FOR 1 POUND OF FIBER

Desired Shade	Light	Medium	Dark
Water	2½ gallons	2½ gallons	2½ gallons
Dye powder	½ tsp	1¾ tsp	3½ tsp
Glauber's salts	1 tbs	1 tbs	1 tbs
White distilled vinegar	1 cup + 6 tbs	1 cup + 6 tbs	1 cup + 6 tbs

Ikat dyer dipping wrapped yarns into cochineal vat outside Antigua, Guatemala, photo Joe Coca.

Ikat in Mexico & Guatemala: A Family Memoir

ALEJANDRO DE ÁVILA

My earliest recollection of ikat goes back to my childhood. Our mother kept a luxurious rebozo from Santa María del Río that our father had presented to her when they got married. It was stored carefully in a locked drawer that I was allowed to open every now and then, only because it also contained a music box that had been sent to me for Christmas by an aunt living in Europe. I would admire the rebozo's tiny dotted pattern and long elaborate fringes **(see facing page)** while listening to "Silent Night." An aura of family treasure shone in the music box and the rebozo: These delicate objects loaded with emotional value were far too precious to be removed from their protective chest of heavy dark wood. Although I had no idea how it was made, ikat in my child's mind was tied to our parents' vows of fidelity, and hence to the security my siblings and I felt as we were growing up.

Years later, the link with family history was strengthened when our grandmother showed me a small, humble rebozo that she kept in loving memory of her daughter Mercedes, who had died tragically as a teenager. Woven out of cotton, the fabric had faded, but the colors remained beautiful and the pattern stood out clearly. The reserve knots had been tied with the utmost care and the dyeing had been done by a master artisan, I began to appreciate. Here was a handsome garment that our father's sister had worn as a little girl. It looked like she had used it for quite a long time. Ikat had been part of our family's everyday social skin only a generation before my own, I realized.

The next discovery came when I visited relatives in the rural region of San Luis Potosí, where our paternal grandfather was born. There I met a cousin of his who still remembered him and who told me stories about our family during the hardships of the Revolution of 1910. Once he heard that I was interested in textiles, he showed me a sash that he had worn as a young man **(shown below)**. I was smitten by that particular weaving, the most beautiful ikat example I had ever seen intended for use by men. To learn that those feathery designs had graced the waists of our relatives just fifty years earlier filled me with delight.

A *cenidor* (men's sash) from El Tepozan, municipality of Cerritos, San Luis Potosí, woven on a backstrap loom around 1920, weft and indigo-dyed warp stripes are industrially spun cotton, red and magenta stripes are rayon, collection of Anacleto Ávila, photo: Alejandro de Ávila.

Detail of a rebozo made in Santa María del Río, state of San Luis Potosí, around 1960, warp and weft of rayon, synthetically dyed, woven on a treadle loom, photo: Alejandro de Ávila.

That same sash was to reveal a secret after a couple of decades, when I came to study textiles in earnest. It dawned on me that the gap in the pattern at the center of the fabric (**see photo below**) conveyed significance: it meant that the warp had been folded before tying the ikat knots, in order to save labor in a process that involved a ring loom. Tubular warps, I began to recognize, are restricted to the area north of the string of volcanoes that dissects our country in two, and surely go back for several centuries. The presence of ikat on a ring loom, I became convinced, is an indication of a long-standing history. My little discovery resonated beyond our family's homeland because much of the literature I had read in Spanish sought to connect rebozos with the textile traditions of the Philippines, India, and Indonesia, as if ikat had arrived in Acapulco on board the Manila galleon one fine day during the colonial period. Our relative's sash made me think otherwise.

Building the collections for the textile museum in Oaxaca, we have been fortunate to acquire outstanding resist-dyed sashes and shawls from various regions in Mexico and Guatemala. Our top ikat treasure is an exceedingly fine rebozo woven with gossamer-thin cotton warps and silk wefts that dates from the late 1800s or early 1900s (**see facing page**). Slightly frayed by wear, it appears to have been put away for many years as a family memento. It seems to have been woven in Calimaya, in the highlands west of Mexico City. The thread count exceeds 90 warps per centimeter (over 230 per inch). The minute design was executed with such skill that the overall pattern conveys a strong horizontal rhythm, even though it's composed of narrow vertical stripes. Respected colleagues who have examined this rebozo consider it to be the finest example they've seen of the art of resist-dyeing, anywhere.

Alejandro de Ávila holds a bachelor's degree in anthropology and physiological psychology from Tulane University, a master's in psychobiology, and a PhD in anthropology from UC Berkeley. He's the founding director of the Oaxaca Ethnobotanical Garden, and the curator and adviser of the Oaxaca Textile Museum. Fascinated by their designs, he began to collect textiles when he was 11 years old; as a teenager, he became an apprentice at a weaving and dyeing workshop.

Detail of a *cenidor* (men's sash), showing the midpoint of the warp, dyed a solid blue with indigo, where the ikat pattern gets reversed. Woven on a ring warp prior to 1970, before the art of ikat died out in local Mexican communities, photo: Alejandro de Ávila.

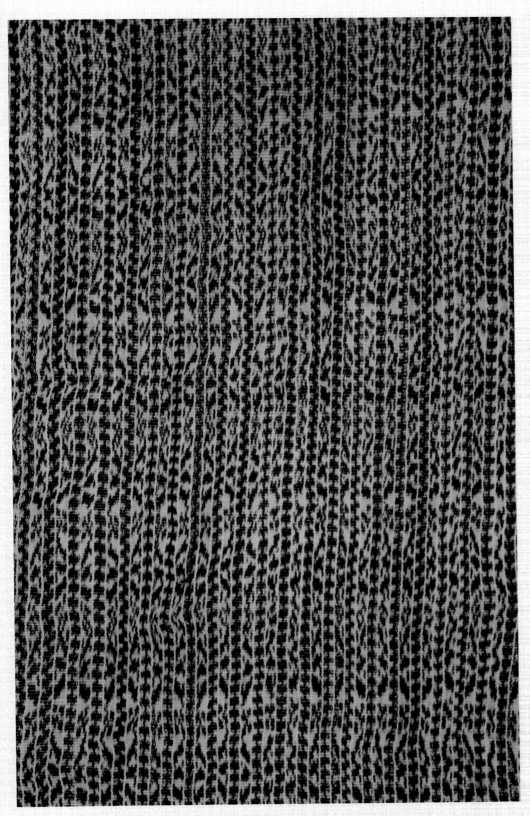

A rebozo detail illustrating the minute scale of the ikat pattern. Design motifs on rebozos are usually negative, i.e., white figures on a dark background; positive designs, as seen on this example, appear to have distinguished the ikat masters of Calimaya, photo: Alejandro de Ávila.

CHAPTER FIVE | the projects

Ikat weaving is fun and fascinating. It's almost magical to see your randomly wrapped resist areas appear and disappear, turning into positive and negative designs and unexpected shifts of color. The scarf, stole, and runner are classic weaving projects, and they are the templates I have selected to illustrate the basics of ikat. The long narrow rectangle provides the perfect canvas for learning because it's easy to weave and manage, compelling to compose, and beautifully emphasizes the graphic drama of feathered dye and shifted fibers.

BEFORE YOU START

Read this short section before you begin. It explains how to work through the projects. As I mentioned in the introduction, this book assumes you have previous experience winding a warp, warping a loom, and weaving yarn into cloth. Every project in this book is based on the simple loom threading of a straight draw, plain weave on four shafts (**figure 1**). Classic warp-ikat design is often best represented or "seen" when woven as simple cloth, literally as warp-faced as you can weave. Warp-ikat designs also show the sought-after ikat contrast when woven as one of the warped-face complex twills.

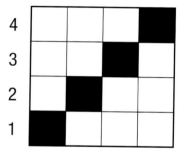

figure 1

I suggest you stick to a simple weave structure in these first projects, as you learn what resist-wrapped yarns do and don't do well. After you're comfortable with stretching, wrapping, dyeing, and "managing" multiple lengths of designed yarn, then go ahead and get complex. You may be surprised to discover that not all of your favorite weave structures are the best choice for showcasing the subtle nuances of your painstaking work at the ikat boards and dyepot. Trial and error will reveal what complex structures do and do not take over and dominate the design field. You don't want the resist-dyed design areas obstructed by a weave structure that steals the thunder from the ikat.

WORK SEQUENTIALLY THROUGH THE BOOK

I recommend that you weave your way through this book from start to finish. Begin with the first very simple project, the Random Wrap Indigo Scarf, and continue to complete the final, more complex Cross+Fire Scarf double-ikat project. The book is laid out so that each project builds upon the previous one, each going a step deeper into the ikat process, sequentially illustrating and building new skill sets one upon the other.

It's very tempting to go overboard and get ahead of yourself on your first ikat project. The project sequence is designed to stand between you and ikat frustration. The seven warp-ikat projects and variations build one upon the other, sequentially teaching specific ikat skill sets. Each project involves many moving parts: fiber selection, design, yarn stretching, resist-wrapping, dyeing, warp-shifting, and, finally, learning the tricks of warping and weaving ikat. Each of these areas is its own complete and unique world, presenting ideas and techniques that may be unfamiliar to you. If the processes at first seem awkward and perhaps even odd, I assure you that you will learn the skill sets quickly. Your confidence and facility will grow exponentially with each project you complete.

READ EACH SET OF INSTRUCTIONS BEFORE STARTING

Each project teaches a new ikat skill requiring specific materials. I don't want you to be caught mid-project without the yarn, tools, or an idea of the time commitment you need to continue.

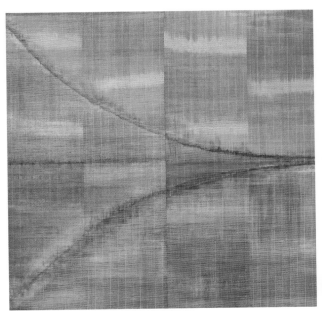

Polly Barton, *Persephone*, 2008, handwoven Japanese *tsumugi* silk double ikat woven in 4 panels, 34 × 72" (86.5 × 183 cm), photo: Wendy McEahern. Using a warp shifter created the stepped horizontal lines in the warp.

Mary Zicafoose, *Women of the World*, 2018, weft-faced ikat diptych tapestry, 87 × 115" (221 × 292 cm) collection of the Womens Center for Advancement, Omaha, NE.

BASIC TOOLKIT

Round up these tools and supplies and keep them in a box together. You'll need them to make every project in this book.

- Pencil
- Graph paper sheets, 8 squares/inch
- Graph paper roll, 2 squares/inch
- Small sharp scissors
- Paper-cutting scissors
- Ruler
- Yardstick
- Tape measure
- Masking tape

BASIC WEAVING EQUIPMENT

You'll need this equipment to make the projects in the book.

- Warping board
- 1 set of loom raddles or DIY ikat boards
- Four 3" (7.5 cm) C-clamps
- Roll of ikat tape or resist-wrapping material
- 2- or 4-shaft loom
- 12- and 15-dent reeds
- Lease sticks
- 2 boat shuttles and bobbins

The projects in this book were all woven on a four-shaft 26" (66 cm) Schacht Baby Wolf floor loom. However, you can weave them on a two-shaft loom, a table loom, a rigid-heddle loom, a tapestry loom, or a loom of different size.

EXPECT DIFFERENCES

While carefully following the project directions in this book, your version of the scarves, stoles, and runners will come out differently than the examples pictured. This isn't due to error. This is the painterly nature of resist-wrapped and dyed fibers when woven into ikat cloth. Your tension and spacing in wrapping resists will be different, your dye measurements and proportions will be slightly different, the degree the dyes seep and bleed beneath and above the resist will be different, as will be your beat and tension at the loom. If I were to weave every project in this book twice, each would resemble the original example, but it would be interestingly different from the first. Ikat creates one-of-a-kind cloth.

THE IKAT RULES

There's a three-word phrase that I write on the board in every ikat workshop that I teach: "The ikat rules." That means that the most important thing about to happen at your loom is spelled I-K-A-T, and it's now the new boss. It means that more than likely we will break a few hallowed and sacred rules of warping, dressing the loom, and weaving, all in the name of making an ikat design fit perfectly and shift beautifully. It also means that you're going to learn some new tricks and do a few things differently than you were taught—only to do it all again a bit differently in the next project.

Ikat is not a technique for the faint of heart. A museum curator once told me that creating ikat cloth demands that you become a visionary, an engineer, and a saint. It involves extreme attention to detail and a high tolerance for risk-taking. Expect planned results as well as surprising accidents to happen to your wrapped yarns while they transform in the dyepot. A technique that by definition requires hand wrapping hundreds, if not thousands of threads, and then dyeing, unwrapping, and collating each and every one of them multiple times before you even approach your loom is a strong contender for the most labor-intensive process … ever.

random wrap indigo scarf

The Random Wrap Indigo Scarf is a simple but mighty first ikat project. It teaches the basics of warp-ikat technique from start to finish. These directions also include two variations on the original project.

IKAT SKILL
The Random Wrap Indigo Scarf teaches how to resist-wrap random warp sections while the warp is on the warping board.

STRUCTURE
Plain weave.

EQUIPMENT
4-shaft loom, 12" (30.5 cm) weaving width; 15-dent reed; lease sticks; 1 boat shuttle.

YARNS
WARP: 5/2 pearl cotton (2,100 yd/lb [4,233 m/kg]; Supreme UKI Astra, Yarn Barn of Kansas), White or Natural, 16 oz (452 g).

WEFT: 30/2 silk (7,850 yd/lb [15,825 m/kg]; Georgia Yarn Company), White, 12 oz (28–56 g).

DYES
Indigo vat for warp and weft.

OTHER SUPPLIES
Basic Toolkit (page 78); warping board; ikat tape or other resist-wrapping materials.

WARP LENGTH
330 ends 3 yd (2.7 m) long (allows 22" [56 cm] for take-up, fringe, and loom waste).

SETTS
WARP: 30 epi (2/dent in a 15-dent reed).

WEFT: 18 ppi.

DIMENSIONS
WIDTH IN LOOM: 11" (28 cm).
WOVEN LENGTH: 89" (226 cm) (measured under tension on the loom).
FINISHED SIZE: 86" × 9½" (218 cm × 24 cm).

NOTES
YARN SELECTION: A warp-dominant weave will emphasize ikat design much more dramatically than a balanced 50-50 weave. 5/2 pearl cotton makes a thick, dense cotton warp paired with 30/2 silk, a light, thin weft.

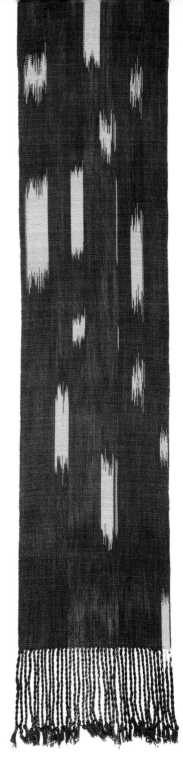

figure 1

figure 2

figure 3

PROCESS

1. USE THE WARPING BOARD AS AN IKAT STRETCHING TOOL. Using 5/2 pearl cotton, measure a total of 330 ends, each 3 yards (2.7 m) long, on a warping board/reel. If your warping board won't comfortably hold 330 ends at one time, stretch the warp in three distinct sections. When the threads begin popping off the pegs, you'll know you've reached full capacity. Wind your warp under even tension and with a cross in place, using the system you're accustomed to. This stretched warp is the perfect canvas for you to begin wrapping random sections of ikat (**figure 1**).

2. WRAP THE WARP. Random wrapping is just that, wrapping yarn with no specific plan in mind. Simply pick up various-sized sections and numbers of warp threads and practice wrapping them using a resist-wrapping material. After several wraps, you'll become more confident and feel like you're getting the hang of it.

Practice making a variety of wraps. Try tying a very tight wrap in a small section and then a very loose wrap in another section. Gather varying numbers of warp threads to form different-sized bundles, and then wrap them in different lengths. Finally, gather an entire width of warp and secure it firmly with a tight thick wrap. You have just created a sampler of random warp wraps (**figure 2**).

3. LABEL. If there's a top or bottom, start or finish, or right or left to your plan, tag, label, and knot, indicating those areas. (Later, after the warp comes out of the dyepot, any subtle clues on the yarn will be virtually unrecognizable.) Check your cross and your warp ties. If they've been tied tightly, they'll also become unintended resist-wraps. Loosen as needed.

4. REMOVE THE WARP FROM THE WARPING BOARD. Some weavers cut the warp ends on the warping board, others don't. I suggest that you not cut the ends but rather run a cotton fabric strip or thick hank of yarn through the warp loop, securing each end of your warp (**figure 3**). This will give you the option to cut or leave your warp in an untouched loop later when dressing the loom.

5. PREPARE THE WEFT YARN. Wind the weft yarn into a skein for dyeing (**figure 4**). Use secure but loose ties to avoid unwanted resists. Alternatively, you could use a commercially dyed yarn, of a similar size, for the weft.

6. DYE. The cotton warp is a cellulose fiber, while the silk weft is protein. Select the dye system of your choice for dyeing. Refer to the instructions to build and use an indigo vat (pages 56–60), and the instructions for dyeing with fiber reactive dye for cellulose and silk (page 64).

7. UNWRAP. After dyeing, carefully unwrap the ikat warp and hang it to dry.

Once unwrapped, the ikat-dyed warp sections are no longer held tightly together, making them more vulnerable and prone to shifting. Stabilize the patterned sections by securing them with masking tape or with a length of ikat tape, to restrict the movement of the threads within each section. This helps prevent the design from spontaneously shifting while handling the yarns as you prepare to dress the loom.

8. WARP THE LOOM. Load your dyed warp sections onto a pair of lease sticks, maintaining the cross in each section. I thread the loom from front to back with the warp ends cut, but you can dress your loom as you've been taught, threading 2 ends per dent in a 15-dent reed, and then one warp end through each heddle in a standard straight draw 1-2-3-4 sequence, on a 4-harness loom.

Do not deliberately shift or organize the warp in any way. What's wrapped and dyed is what you'll weave. Simply tie or loop your warp onto the back warp-beam rod, as you would normally do. Some of the warp threads will stay together and appear to be grouped, and some will naturally shift. Wind on the entire warp, placing a protective roll of paper or sticks between the layers of threads to prevent them from building up directly on top of each other (**figure 5**). Tie onto the front beam.

9. WEAVE. Weave in the header of your choice, allowing 6–8" (15–20.5 cm) for fringe (**figure 6**). I begin and end my scarves, stoles, and runners with a basic hem stitch while on the loom.

Your choice of weft will have a strong and obvious effect on the warp. If you don't like the result of your selection, experiment using other threads in your stash. Weaving should go quickly and smoothly with a boat shuttle. It's exciting to watch the ikat sections emerge and then disappear! When the scarf is completed, cut it off the loom and finish with the fringe style of your choice.

Now you're ready to progress on to weaving the variations.

figure 4

figure 5

figure 6

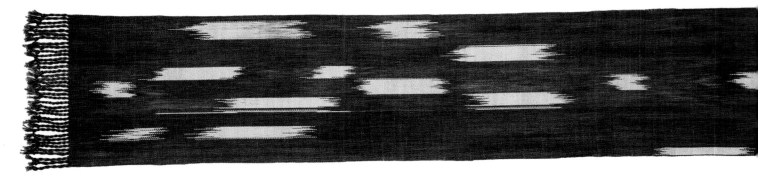

RANDOM WRAP INDIGO SCARF IN SILK

The very fluid pattern on this scarf was achieved by randomly wrapping many more sections of warp than in the previous project and by allowing the slippery nature of the silk to naturally shift the threads while warping the loom.

STRUCTURE

Plain weave.

EQUIPMENT

4-shaft loom, 12" (30.5 cm) weaving width; 15-dent reed; lease sticks; 1 boat shuttle.

YARNS

WARP: 20/2 silk (4,900 yd/lb [10,100 m/kg]; Georgia Yarn Company), White, 4 oz (114 g).

WEFT: 30/2 silk (7,850 yd/lb [15, 010 m/kg]; Georgia Yarn Company), White, 1–2 oz (28–56 g).

DYES

Indigo-dyed warp and weft. Alternatively, you can use a different dye system and/or a commercially dyed weft yarn of similar size.

OTHER SUPPLIES

Basic Toolkit (page 78); warping board; ikat tape or other resist-wrapping materials.

WARP LENGTH

330 ends 3 yd (2.7 m) long (allows 22" [56 cm] for take-up, fringe, and loom waste).

SETTS

WARP: 30 epi (2/dent in a 15-dent reed).

WEFT: 18 ppi.

NOTES

YARN SELECTION: Use two weights of silk: 20/2 for the warp, 30/2 for the weft. When dyeing the warp, remember to also wind and dye the weft yarn.

PROCESS

For this variation, use the same weaving directions as in the first project.

FRINGE DESIGN

Do you want the fringes of your scarf to carry an ikat pattern or be the solid color of your warp? I was interested in what a dyed ikat fringe might look like on this scarf, so I resist-wrapped the warp on the warping board from one end to the other. Should you want your fringe dyed a solid color, do not resist-wrap the beginning and end of the warp that will be used in tie-on, fringe, and loom waste.

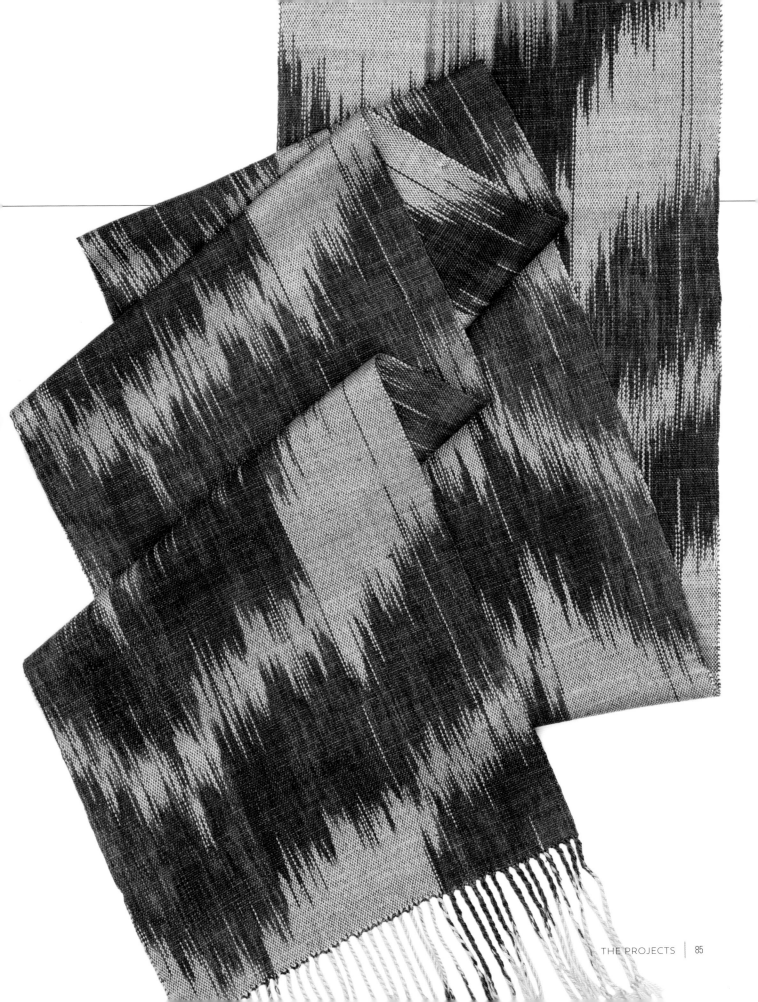

RANDOM WRAP INDIGO SCARVES IN WOOL WITH BORDERS

This version of the Random Wrap Indigo Scarf continues to explore different resist-wrapping techniques for interesting woven effects: tight wrap, loose wrap, full hank wrap, sectional wrap. It presents three changes in procedure. The first involves stretching a warp for two scarves, rather than one; the second adjusts the dye system to partner with wool, a protein fiber. The third introduces borders: both undyed warp yarns and dyed warp yarns without ikat resists.

STRUCTURE
Plain weave.

EQUIPMENT
4-shaft loom, 12" (30.5 cm) weaving width; 15-dent reed; lease sticks; 1 boat shuttle.

YARNS
WARP: 18/2 JaggerSpun Superfine Merino (100% Merino wool, 5,040 yd/lb; [10,388 m/kg]), White, 5 oz (142 g).

WEFT: (Variation #1) 20/2 pearl cotton (8,400 yd/lb [16,950 m/kg]; Supreme UKI, Yarn Barn of Kansas), White, 1 oz (28 g).

(Variation #2) 1 oz (28 g) 60/2 Valley Yarns silk (100% silk; 14,800 yd/lb [30,028 m/kg]; WEBS), Pacific #646, 1 oz (28 g).

YOU'LL USE A DIFFERENT WEFT YARN FOR EACH SCARF: a fine 20/2 pearl cotton that will be dyed in indigo for Variation #1 and a 60/2 silk commercially dyed blue-green for Variation #2. The different shade of blue and the luster of the commercially dyed silk create a subtle but startling influence when woven with the indigo-dyed wool warp.

DYES
Indigo vat for warp and for the weft of one scarf.

OTHER SUPPLIES
Basic Toolkit (page 78); warping board; ikat tape or other resist-wrapping materials.

WARP LENGTH
312 ends, 5½ yd long (5 m) (allows 33" [84 cm] for take-up, fringe, and loom waste), for 2 scarves.

SETTS
WARP: 24 epi (2/dent in a 12-dent reed).

WEFT: Scarf 1–20 ppi; Scarf 2–30 ppi.

DIMENSIONS
WIDTH IN LOOM: 13" (33 cm).
WOVEN LENGTH: each scarf measures 72" (183 cm) (measured under tension on the loom).

Random Wrap Indigo Scarf in Wool,
Variation #1 with Cotton

PROCESS

This Random Wrap Indigo Scarf variation involves winding a longer warp, allowing you to complete two scarves. This will give you practice visualizing, planning, and doing the math to measure off areas of loom waste and fringe for both scarves indicating where the warp will be resist-wrapped.

Mark the "blank areas" (the space in between the two scarves where the fringes will be located and the loom waste) on the stretched warp with a thread of a different color, chalk, or masking tape. The warp will be resist-wrapped in the body of the scarf.

1. WIND THE WARP. The borders on this scarf require that the warp be wound in three different sections, as shown in the chart below:

a. The ikat warp: Wind 240 ends.

b. Dyed borders: Wind two different warp sections, 12 threads each, to be placed on the outside selvedges. These will be dyed without any resists.

c. White borders: Wind two different warp sections, 24 threads each, to be placed on each border. These will not be dyed but the yarns must be treated in a similar way to the dyed yarns to assure even shrinkage throughout the scarf. They can be scoured with the ikat warp. If using a heated dyebath, these yarns should go into a clean, heated bath as well (no dye). If one section of your ikat shrinks markedly more than the others, your design will be altered, particularly when using a fiber extremely prone to shrinkage, such as wool.

Dyed border	White border	Ikat warp	White border	Dyed border
12	24	240	24	12

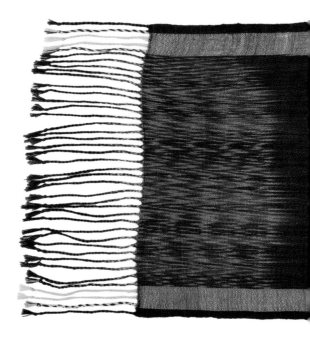

2. WRAP. Wrap the ikat warp for Variation #1 in random sections, simply dividing the warp up into small interesting areas and wrapping.

Wrap Variation #2 entirely using the whole hank method. Gather sections of the full width of the warp on the warping board and wrap, some tightly, some loosely. The girth of the wrap creates an entirely different woven effect. Thick bundles of wrapped yarn encourage the dye to wick up under the ikat tape in the dyepot, creating a much more painterly and shifted pattern.

3. DYE THE WEFT YARN. Wind the cotton yarns for Variation #1 into a skein for dyeing. Both protein and cellulose fibers can be successfully dyed in indigo.

4. THREAD THE LOOM AND WEAVE. Arrange the warp sections with borders on either side. Use a straight draw sequence. Weave in your header, allowing 6–8" (15–20.5 cm) for fringe.

Note: Further explorations can be made with random warp ikats by experimenting with weft yarns. Use different colors, weights of yarn, and fibers. You might also tie up your treadles for different twill sequences and see if you like the results.

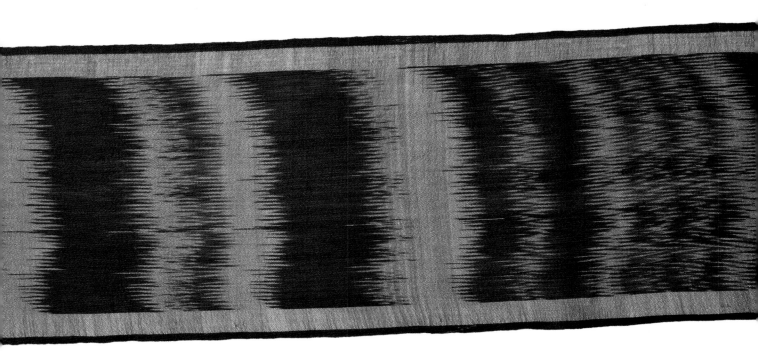

Random Wrap Indigo Scarf in Wool, Variation #2 with Silk

shifted-warp scarf: chevrons

This project introduces variations on warp-shifting techniques used worldwide to create and dramatize resist-dye patterns on ikat warps. Warp-shifting is accomplished while warping the loom. This book illustrates four methods of warp-shifting. The staggered knot system is taught in this project. Staggered cords on a dowel is used in the Checkerboard Stole project. The simple dowel shift is used in the Shifted-Warp Scarf: Arrows variation, and the Mediterranean Stole and Byzantine Arrows projects introduce a wooden shifting device.

IKAT SKILL

Teaches how to create shifted-warp designs from very simple resist-wrapped design elements with staggered knots: tying small bundles of the dyed warps in different staggered lengths directly onto the back-beam rod of the loom.

STRUCTURE

Plain weave.

EQUIPMENT

4-shaft loom, 16" (41 cm) weaving width; 12-dent reed; lease sticks; 1 boat shuttle.

YARNS

WARP: 20/2 Normandy Linen (wet-spun line flax, 3,000 yd/lb [6,050 m/kg]; Yarn Barn of Kansas), Bleached Ivory, 6 oz (170 g).

WEFT: 20/2 silk (5,000 yd/lb [10,000 m/kg]; Georgia Yarn Company), White, 2 oz (60 g) or a commercially dyed yarn of similar size

DYES

Indigo vat for warp and weft, or dye of your choice.

OTHER SUPPLIES

Basic Toolkit (page 78); warping board; ikat tape or other resist-wrapping materials.

WARP LENGTH

312 ends 3 yd (2.7 m) long (allows 33" [84 cm] for take-up, fringe, ikat shifting, and loom waste).

SETTS

WARP: 24 epi (2/dent in a 12-dent reed).

WEFT: 20 ppi.

DIMENSIONS

WIDTH IN THE REED: 13" (33 cm).

WOVEN LENGTH: 79" (201 cm) (measured under tension on the loom).

FINISHED SIZE: 75" × 11¼" (191 cm × 29 cm).

PROCESS

1. WIND THE WARP AND WRAP. Wind the warp on the warping board in three equal sections of 104 warp ends each. Loosely tie off each distinct section and keep all three sections on the warping board. Resist-wrap each section individually as a separate design unit. The sample scarf was tied in resist-wraps approximately 4" (10 cm) long and spaced equally 3–4" (8–10 cm) apart for the length of each warp section. Determine whether you want the fringe dyed or resist-wrapped.

2. PREPARE THE WEFT YARN. Wind the silk weft yarns into a skein for dyeing unless you're using commercially dyed weft yarn.

3. DYE. Use indigo or the dye system of your choice. After dyeing, carefully remove the ikat wraps but leave the loose ties for each warp bundle in place. Dry the warp yarns.

4. ADJUST YARNS TO CREATE A SHIFTED DESIGN. Place the three dyed sections of ikat warp on lease sticks and secure them to the front beam of your loom (**figure 1**). Leave the loose ties for each warp bundle in place. Thread 2 ends per dent in a 12-dent reed, through the heddles in a standard 1-2-3-4 draw.

For this project you'll pull, adjust, and then tie small groups of warp threads onto the back beam, adjusting the ikat-dyed threads from each warp group to create a shifting flame pattern. This will require dividing each warp group into an odd number of thread groupings—three, five, or seven—for each of the three design areas. I stabilize my small groups of warp threads by tying them with an overhand knot first. Then, I manually tug and pull the tied groups of warp threads to create a staggered pattern as I tie them onto the back beam (**figures 2 and 3**).

Once all the groups are tied on, comb through the warp with your fingers and pull it under tension to determine if the shifting is pleasing to you (**figure 4**). If not, simply undo and re-tie the warp bundles that are messy or out of design sequence. Continue to carefully comb through the warp as you wind it onto the back beam to achieve even tensioning (**figure 4**). Tie onto the front beam.

5. WEAVE. Weave enough header to allow for a finishing with a fringe; 6–7" (15–18 cm) is adequate. I encourage you to experiment with different weft colors and yarns, and border treatments—perhaps warp stripes as in the Three-Striped Runner (page 98). See what details strengthen the ikat. The weft yarn doesn't need to be the same color, size, or manufacturer as the warp. The finer the weft yarn, the more vivid your ikat will appear.

Congratulations, you've successfully finished this scarf. Now for the next variation, a larger format and a bit more complex. Your skills are growing!

figure 1

figure 2

figure 3

figure 4

VARIATION

SHIFTED-WARP SCARF: ARROWS

In this process, you'll use a wooden dowel as a shifting tool. It works like a very simplified version of a Japanese shifting box that has dowels at different levels to shift the warp. The resist-dyed threads create a simple shifted pattern easily achieved by tying alternating sections of the warp bundles onto a wooden dowel that is lashed to the warp beam, as well as tying bundles directly onto the warp beam itself. The warp is comprised of ikat-dyed threads, dyed threads (no ikat), and undyed threads.

YARNS

WARP: 20/2 Normandy Linen (wet-spun line flax, 3,000 yd/lb [6,050 m/kg]; Yarn Barn of Kansas), Unbleached Ivory, 6 oz (170 g).

WEFT: 60/2 Valley Yarns silk (100% silk, 15,000 yd/lb [30,028 m/kg]; WEBS), Pacific #646, 1 oz (30 g).

WARP LENGTH

322 total ends, 3 yd (2.7 m) long (allows 33" [84 cm] for take-up, fringe, ikat shifting, and loom waste). Ikat resisted and dyed: 144 threads. Dyed but no resist: 84 threads. No dye: 84 threads.

SETTS

WARP: 24 epi (2/dent in a 12-dent reed).
WEFT: 20 ppi.

DIMENSIONS

WIDTH IN THE REED: 13" (33 cm).
WOVEN LENGTH: 79" (201 cm) (measured under tension on the loom).
FINISHED SIZE: 75" × 11¼" (190 cm × 29 cm).

NOTES

In addition to the usual weaving equipment, you'll need a wooden dowel ½–1" (1.3–2.5 cm) in diameter, cut at least 1" (2.5 cm) longer than the warp width but shorter than the back-beam rod.

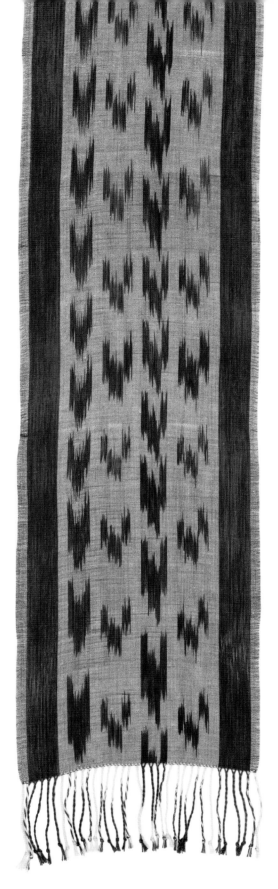

PROCESS

1. WIND THE WARP AND WRAP. The warp will be prepared in three different parts. Wind the warp to be ikat resisted on the warping board in four equal sections of 36 warp ends each. Loosely tie off each distinct section and keep all three sections on the warping board. Resist-wrap each section individually as a separate design unit. Wind the other two sections of warp. Be sure to treat the undyed warp in the same scour bath to ensure that shrinkage will be the same as the other warp threads.

2. DYE. Use the dye system of your choice. The example shown was dyed with indigo.

Carefully remove the ikat wraps but leave the loose ties for each warp bundle in place. Dry the warp yarns.

3. THREAD THE LOOM. To begin this process of shifting warp threads with the assistance of a dowel, thread the loom, placing the dyed sections of ikat warp on lease sticks, and secure to the front beam of your loom. Use the chart below as a guide to thread placement. Thread 2 ends per dent in a 12-dent reed, and through the heddles in a standard 1-2-3-4 draw.

No dye	Solid dye	No dye	Ikat	No dye	Ikat	No dye	Ikat	No dye	Ikat	No dye	Solid dye	No dye
12	42	12	36	12	36	12	36	12	36	12	42	12

4. SHIFT THE IKAT. This project creates a two-step staggered pattern. Accomplish this shift by securely lashing the wooden dowel to the back-beam rod of the loom (**figure 1**). Leave space between the two rods, enough that you can get your fingers between them. This dowel serves as an extension to the back-beam rod and will stay in place for the entire warping and weaving process. The larger the space between the rods, the more the warp will shift.

By alternately tying the ikat warp bundles onto the back beam and the lashed dowel, a shifting of the ikat threads will take place. For instance, take a group of 36 ikat-dyed threads. Divide that into 3 equal groups and tie a small over-hand knot at the end of each group to keep the threads together. Attach the middle group to the large dowel. Tie the other two groups to the regular back-beam rod. This will automatically shift the middle threads. After all of the warp groups are tied onto one bar or the other, comb through the warp and pull it under tension to determine if you like the way the shifting looks. If not, just undo and re-tie the warp bundles to suit your taste. Continue to carefully comb through the warp as you wind it onto the back beam. Tie onto the front beam.

5. WEAVE. This scarf was woven with commercially dyed silk yarn. Feel free to dye your own weft if you prefer.

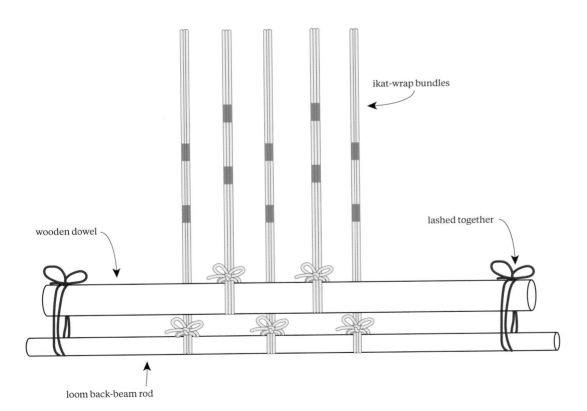

ikat-wrap bundles

lashed together

wooden dowel

loom back-beam rod

figure 1

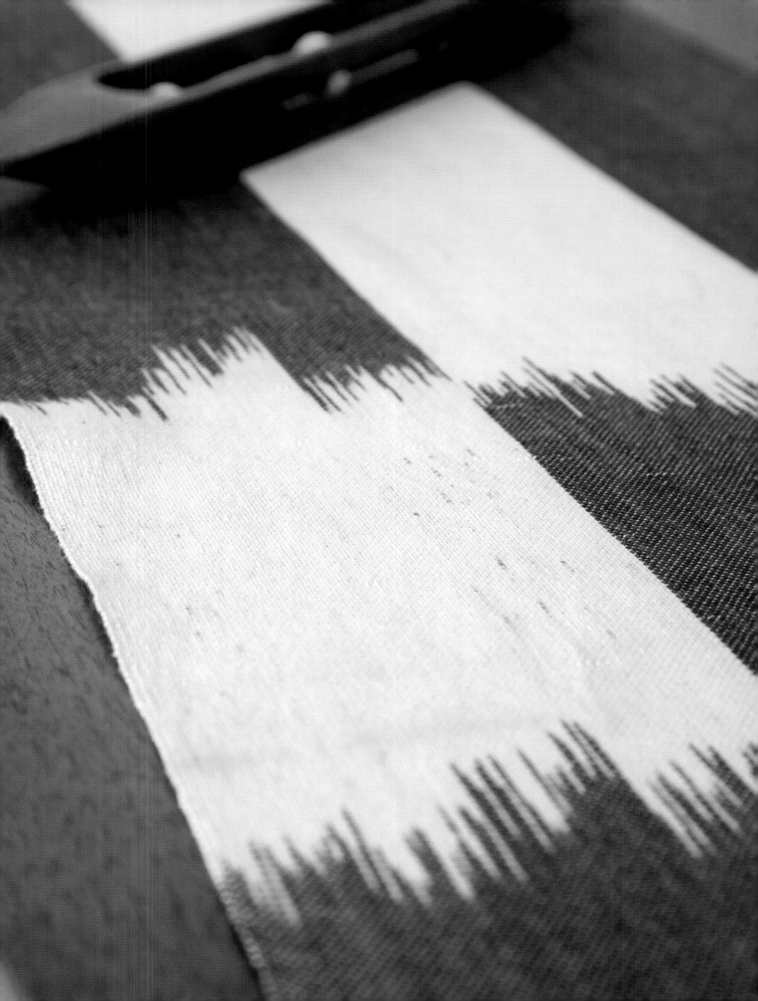

three-striped runner

This project illustrates techniques for wrapping long and large design areas. The long ikat warp stripes for this runner are not wrapped on the warping board, requiring a different approach to stretching and wrapping. The weft in this runner is not dyed, resulting in the bright white areas of pattern.

IKAT SKILL

This project introduces a new system of stretching and wrapping the warp, and the use of a working sketch and a full-size cartoon to define areas of resist. After the warp is wound on the warping board, it is removed from the board to a table where it is placed under tension, stretched between ikat boards or raddles. The cartoon guide is positioned underneath the warp and defines where the warp ties will be placed. The ikat is not intentionally shifted.

STRUCTURE

Plain weave.

EQUIPMENT

4-shaft loom, 16" (41 cm) weaving width; 12-dent reed; lease sticks; 1 boat shuttle.

YARNS

WARP: 5/2 pearl cotton (2,100 yd/lb [4,238 m/kg]; Supreme UKI Astra, Yarn Barn of Kansas), White, 9 oz (255 g).

WEFT: 20/2 pearl cotton (8,400 yd/lb [16,950 m/kg]; Supreme UKI, Yarn Barn of Kansas), Natural, 2 oz (57 g).

WARP LENGTH

360 ends 3 yd (2.7 m) long (allows 32" [81 cm] for take-up, fringe, and loom waste).

DYES

Indigo vat for warp only.

OTHER EQUIPMENT

Basic Toolkit (page 78); 2 raddles of similar size, or 2 ikat boards; 4 C-clamps, 3" (7.5 cm); ikat tape or other resist-wrapping materials.

SETTS

WARP: 24 epi (2/dent in a 12-dent reed).

WEFT: 18 ppi.

DIMENSIONS

WIDTH IN THE REED: 15" (38 cm).
WOVEN LENGTH: 90" (228 cm) (measured under tension on the loom).
FINISHED SIZE: 87" × 13½" (221 cm × 34 cm).

NOTES

The warp and weft for the Three-Striped Runner were chosen specifically to produce a dense warp face weave and give the cloth a firm hand suitable for a table runner. This warp was measured on the warping board in three separate sections.

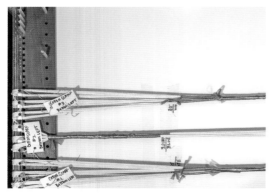

120 120 120

Distribute the warp
over nine pegs,
three pegs per section

figure 1: The working sketch (left),
and a variation drawn on graph paper (right).

PROCESS

1. PREPARING THE WARP. Wind the warp on the warping board in 3 separate sections of 120 threads each. Subdivide each of these three sections into 40 thread groups and loosely tie off each one to keep them in order. *Do not* cut the ends when the warp is removed from the boards. The loops will be used to secure the warp sections to the pegs on the stretcher boards affixed to the table.

2. STRETCH THE WARP OFF THE WARPING BOARD. For the first time, we are using a system of stretching the warp that is *not* the warping board. Choose the off-board system of your preference: 2 raddles or DIY ikat boards (refer to Methods, page 34). Secure each board to opposite ends of the table with a pair of C-clamps.

Make a working sketch for creating long simple stripes (my working sketch, as well as a variation, is shown in **figure 1**). There's no need to make a full-size cartoon for a simple design like this. Just mark on the table with masking tape to indicate starting and stopping points for the resist-wrapping (**figure 2**). Move the premeasured warp to your raddle or ikat board system and distribute the warp over 9 pegs/nails stretched between two ikat boards placed at each end of the table. Adjust the tension for wrapping. Refer to the masking tape on the table as a guide for the ikat wrapping. The ikat wraps are staggered to give a painterly feathered illusion to the ikat. If I wanted a harder

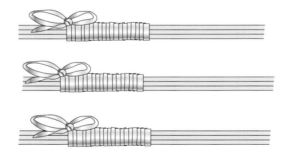

figure 3

figure 2

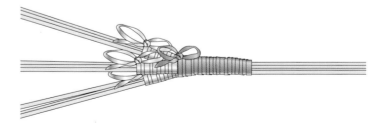

figure 4

edge to the dyed area, I would wrap evenly to the edge of the masking tape (see Methods, Step 3 on page 40).

3. WRAP THE RESIST AREAS. Long wraps are managed by "adding on" ikat tape as you run out. Rather than tying a knot midway in a long section to be wrapped, overlap the short end of tape with a new long strip and continue wrapping (refer to Methods, page 41).

When large bundles of warp are wrapped together, the dye is likely to wick underneath the wrapping. To keep clean resists and expedite the wrapping process, begin to wrap each of the 40 thread bundles individually for 1 or 2" (2.5–5 cm), as shown in figure 3. Then gather all three of the small bundles and wrap the remaining lengths of the sections together, overlapping the wrap (**figure** 4).

4. DYE. Dye the warp. After carefully unwrapping the dyed yarns, bind and secure the design areas together in a few places with a length of ikat tape or masking tape to prevent extensive warp-shifting during the yarn handling. Dry the yarns.

5. THREAD THE LOOM. As you thread, make sure to keep the resist-dyed areas of the design compressed together and not excessively shifted, unless that's your plan. You control the degree of shift in the threading and tying-on process. Aligning and organizing resist-dyed ikat warp threads is not a mindless process and requires more "fussing" than randomly threading the loom. (For a definition of fussing, see page 129.)

Instead of completely threading the loom from front beam to back beam, you can tie new warp threads onto an existing warp of similar sett and thread count. Sometimes this is a time-saver, sometimes not. This helps keep all the threads even and also provides another opportunity for warp-shifting small groups of threads (**figure** 5).

6. WEAVE. The feathered ikat edges juxtaposed with the long, bold stripes create a surprising and pleasing effect (**figure** 6). When in doubt, stripes always work.

Should you want to tie on another warp, be sure to leave long enough ends for tying on in the cutting-off process. Secure the remaining warp in tied bundles so the ends don't fall through the reed (**figure** 7).

figure 5

figure 6

figure 7

checkerboard stole: tencel

The Checkerboard Stole is a more complex project that involves planning, making a full-size cartoon, and the use of a two-board system for yarn stretching and wrapping. The ikat boards are clamped to opposite sides of a long table. The entire warp needs to be exposed, so if your table is not long enough, stretch the warp over two tables. The cartoon is secured between the boards, and the measured warp sections are distributed in correct design sequence spaced between the pegs on the ikat board. Warp-shifting is achieved by using the staggered cord shifting method onto the back beam.

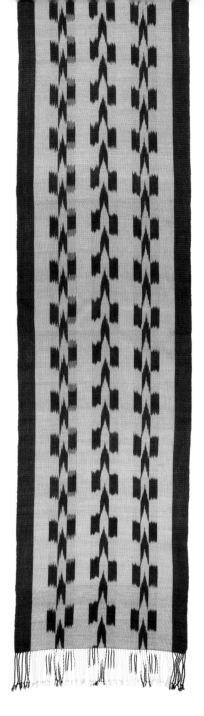

IKAT SKILL
This project involves making and using a full-size cartoon as a wrapping guide for an ikat warp. A new warp-shifting system is introduced: staggered cords on the back-beam rod.

STRUCTURE
Plain weave.

EQUIPMENT
4-shaft loom, 22" (56 cm) weaving width; 15-dent reed; lease sticks; 1 boat shuttle.

YARNS
WARP: 8/2 Tencel (3,360 yd/lb [7,378 m/kg]; WEBS), White, 18 oz (510 g).

WEFT: 20/2 pearl cotton (8,400 yd/lb [16,934 m/kg]; Supreme UKI, Yarn Barn of Kansas), White, 2 oz (57 g).

DYES
Indigo vat for warp and weft.

OTHER SUPPLIES
Basic Toolkit (page 78); Kraft paper, 68½ × 18¾" (174 × 48 cm); set of raddles or ikat boards; 4 C-clamps, 3" (7.5 cm); ikat tape or other resist-wrapping material.

WARP LENGTH
600 ends 3 yd (2.7 m) long (allows 34" [86 cm] for take-up, fringe, loom waste, ikat shifting).

SETTS
WARP: 30 epi (2/dent in a 15-dent reed).
WEFT: 20 pp.

DIMENSIONS
WIDTH IN THE REED: 20" (51 cm).
WOVEN LENGTH: 74" (188 cm) (measured under tension on the loom).
FINISHED SIZE: 68½" × 18¾" (174 cm × 48 cm).

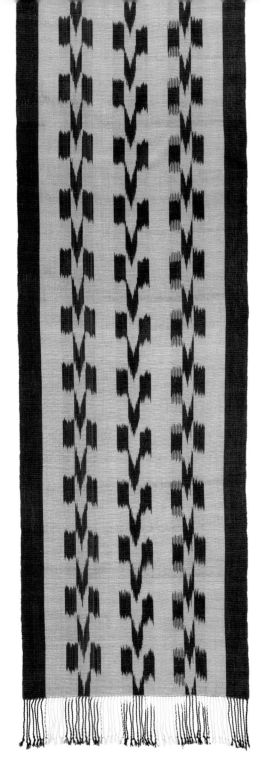

PROCESS

1. PREPARE AND WRAP THE WARP. Here's the warping sequence on the warping board:

▸ Wind two individual sections of warp for the border, each 2" (5 cm) wide or 60 ends; label them to be dyed in indigo. TOTAL ENDS: 120. TOTAL SECTIONS: 2

▸ Wind and label four individual warp sections that will be the white stripes between the shifted ikat design, 1¾" (4.5 cm) or 52 ends. These won't be dyed. TOTAL ENDS: 208. TOTAL SECTIONS: 4

▸ Wind and label nine individual sections of warp each 1" (2.5 cm) wide, or 30 ends. Each of these sections will be wrapped and dyed in a later step and then shifted when warping the loom. TOTAL ENDS: 270. TOTAL SECTIONS: 9

▸ TOTAL END COUNT: 598. TOTAL SECTION COUNT: 15

Another way to break down the warp preparation is with a chart indicating the number of threads in each section, as shown below.

2. CREATE A CARTOON. You can download, print, and assemble the cartoon for my design at www.interweave.com/IkatCartoons, or design your own cartoon for the stole, drawing it full-size on Kraft paper and indicating the areas to be resist-wrapped.

3. STRETCH AND WRAP THE YARNS. Attach the ikat boards or raddles to opposite ends of the table with C-clamps. Using masking tape, secure the cartoon on the table, between the ikat boards. Distribute the individual warp design sections on the ikat boards in order. Space the warp sections to match the pattern. Following the cartoon, resist-wrap every area that is marked. There's no need to stretch the warp sections that won't be dyed (**figure 1**).

4. WIND THE WEFT, LABEL, AND DYE. Wind weft yarn into a skein if you choose to dye it. Otherwise use a commercially dyed yarn of similar size.

Solid color dye	No dye	Ikat dye	Ikat dye	Ikat dye	No dye	Ikat dye	Ikat dye	Ikat dye	No dye	Ikat dye	Ikat dye	Ikat dye	No dye	Solid color dye
60	52	30	30	30	52	30	30	30	52	30	30	30	52	60

Place the individual warp sections on a table in the sequence they'll be woven. Label everything. Remove the four white sections that are not to be dyed. Scour the remaining nine wrapped sections and two border sections to prepare for dyeing, then dye them. Remember to scour the white sections separately so that the shrinkage will be the same as the rest of the warp.

When dyeing is complete, remove the ties and dry the yarns.

5. WARP THE LOOM. Load and arrange the individual warp sections onto the lease sticks, following the design sequence in the cartoon. My design sequence is as follows: dyed border, white stripe, 3 sections of wrapped ikat, white stripe, 3 sections of wrapped ikat, white stripe, 3 sections of wrapped ikat, white stripe, dyed border (**figure 2**). If you've used your own cartoon, your sequence may be different.

Thread the warp ends through the reed and heddles, securing the ikat areas with masking tape to prevent further shifting.

6. SHIFT THE IKAT. You'll shift only the center element of the three wrapped ikat sections that make up the ikat design stripes on the stole. There are three similar areas to shift.

Subdivide each of the three center sections into an odd number of smaller warp bundles. Line up the ikat ends and secure each small unit with a knot. Create the shifted pattern by attaching the three five-bundle sections to the back beam using the staggered cord shifting method (**figure 3**). You can find more information on staggered cord ties on page 26.

7. WEAVE. Weave the runner with the dyed weft or a commercially dyed yarn of similar size.

Now that you've completed this stole, and tried a new warp-shifting technique, why not make the variation that starts on the next page?

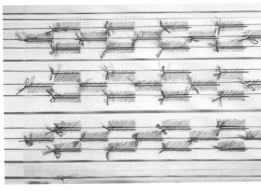

figure 1

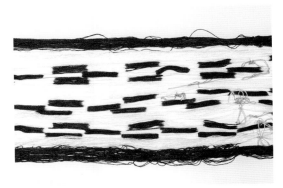

figure 2

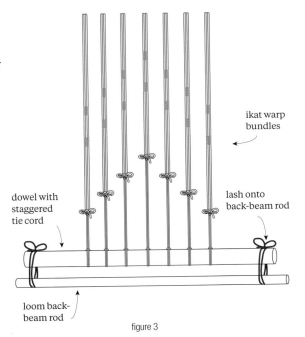

ikat warp bundles

dowel with staggered tie cord

lash onto back-beam rod

loom back-beam rod

figure 3

CHECKERBOARD STOLE: COTTON

For centuries, ikat makers around the world have streamlined their processes down to techniques that resulted in the greatest design impact for the least number of wraps. This explains the many repeat design patterns within a piece of woven ikat cloth. This version of the Checkerboard Stole uses the same cartoon as the first but introduces a more efficient wrapping technique for repeating a design motif.

STRUCTURE
Plain weave.

EQUIPMENT
4-shaft loom, 22" (56 cm) weaving width; 15-dent reed; lease sticks; 1 boat shuttle.

YARNS
WARP: 20/2 pearl cotton (8,400 yd/lb [16,950 m/kg]; Supreme UKI, Yarn Barn of Kansas), White, 4 oz (114 g).

WEFT: 20/2 pearl cotton (8,400 yd/lb [16,950 m/kg]; Supreme UKI, Yarn Barn of Kansas), White, 2 oz (57 g).

DYES
Indigo vat for warp and weft

OTHER SUPPLIES
Basic Toolkit (page 78); set of raddles or ikat boards; 4 C-clamps, 3" (7.5 cm); ikat tape or other resist-wrapping material.

WARP LENGTH
600 ends 3 yd (2.7 m) long (allows 34" [86 cm] for take-up, fringe, loom waste, ikat shifting).

SETTS
WARP: 30 epi (2/dent in a 15-dent reed).
WEFT: 30 ppi.

DIMENSIONS
WIDTH IN THE REED: 20" (51 cm).
WOVEN LENGTH: 74" (188 cm) (measured under tension on the loom).
FINISHED SIZE: 68½" × 18¾" (174 cm × 47.5 cm).

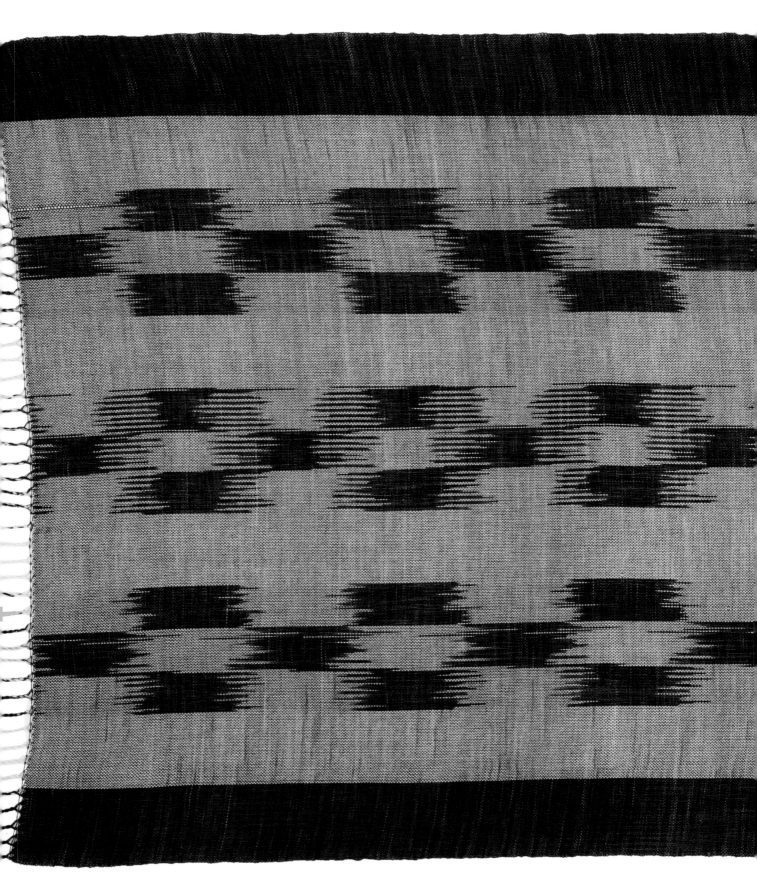

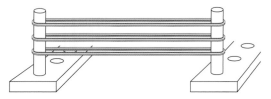

figure 1

figure 2

PROCESS

1. PREPARE THE WARP. Follow the procedure for winding the warp described in Checkerboard Stole: Tencel (page 104). Measure and label the same small bundles of warp for specific design sections.

2. STRETCH AND WRAP THE YARNS. Set up your ikat boards on a table; however, take the following shortcut. Rather than distributing each of the nine sections of warp to be wrapped between the teeth of the raddles in nine sections, simply layer and stack up all of the sections of similar design one on top of the other (**figure 1**). Tension these between two opposing pegs on the stretching boards. That means three sections of warp are stretched on top of each other on three pegs rather than singly on nine pegs. Each layer is an individually contained and labeled warp section so there's no fear of mix-up. Gather the layers together and wrap them as one unit (**figure 2**), following your cartoon.

3. DYE THE WARP AND WEFT. Carefully remove the ties and dry the yarns.

4. WARP THE LOOM. After dyeing and unwrapping, load the individual warp sections onto the lease sticks in their proper design order and dress the loom. In this version of the stole, the ikat-wrapped warp sections were not deliberately shifted so any patterning that occurred was due to the natural shift that happens when yarns get handled. Of course, you may deliberately shift and tug the yarns to create patterns (**figure 3**). Or use the dowel shifting method and alternately distribute and tie ikat warp bundles between the back-beam rod and the dowel. This will create a rhythmical and easy automatic shifted-warp pattern.

5. WEAVE. Weave the stole with the dyed yarn or a commercially dyed yarn of similar size (**figure 4**).

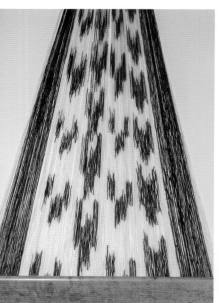

figure 3

figure 4

mediterranean stole

This project began with a rough sketch that was turned into a more refined working sketch (to scale) on graph paper, and finally became a plan for warping and resisting the ikat.

Warp-shifting devices are popular tools in Asian weaving. They are simple tools for creating shifted-warp patterns. The center section of the shifted-warp-ikat design on this stole is created using a DIY wooden shifting tool attached to the back beam of the loom, rather than by using one of the hand-knotted warp-shifting methods previously introduced.

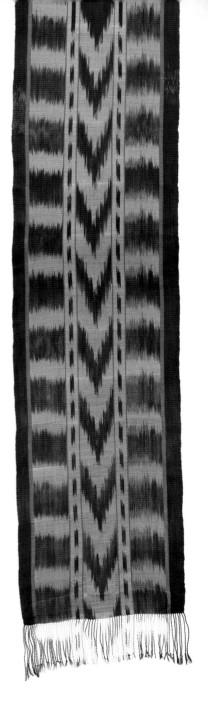

IKAT SKILL
This project introduces you to very simple ikat measuring and wrapping templates made from cardboard and the warp-shifting device attached to the back beam of the loom to create shifted-warp patterns when tying on the warp.

STRUCTURE
Plain weave.

EQUIPMENT
4-shaft loom, 24" (61 cm) weaving width; 15-dent reed; lease sticks; 1 boat shuttle.

YARNS
WARP: 8/2 Tencel (3,360 yd/lb [7,378 m/kg]; WEBS), White, 18 oz (510 g); Lemongrass, 2 oz (57 g).

WEFT: 60/2 Valley Yarns silk (100% silk, 15,000 yd/lb [30,028 m/kg]; WEBS), Pacific #646, 2 oz (57 g).

DYES
Indigo vat for warp; dye materials and auxiliaries.

OTHER SUPPLIES
Basic Toolkit (page 78); 1 set of raddles or ikat boards; 4 C-clamps, 3" (7.5 cm); wooden warp-shifting device (see page 152 for directions on making one); 3 pieces of cardboard, approximately 3 × 12" (7.5 × 30.5 cm) to serve as ikat-tying guides; ikat tape or other resist-wrapping material.

WARP LENGTH
600 ends 4 yd (3.7 m) long (allows 33" [84 cm] for take-up, fringe, and loom waste).

SETTS
WARP: 30 epi (2/dent in a 15-dent reed).

WEFT: 20 ppi.

DIMENSIONS
WIDTH IN THE REED: 20" (51 cm).
WOVEN LENGTH: 87" (221 cm) (measured under tension on the loom).
FINISHED SIZE: 84" × 19" (213 cm × 48 cm).

PROCESS

1. PLAN THE DESIGN. You can either download, print, and assemble the cartoon for this project, which is online at www.interweave.com/IkatCartoons, or create your own design by doing something similar to my approach: I roughly sketched out a design on the back of an envelope (**figure 1**) and then drew it to scale on graph paper (**figure 2**). The goal was to create a balanced but lively design. Sketching in the pattern areas, I selected and repeated three ikat design elements: the bar, the small square, and a shifted ikat chevron to be highlighted in the center of the stole. I decided to add solid white stripes and a few warps of commercially dyed Tencel as an accent color.

The scale drawing helped me determine the number of threads and the length of the ikat resists and dyed areas and make a plan for winding the different warp sections, as shown in the chart below. If you're not following my design, create your own chart.

2. WIND THE WARP. To measure your warp, simply follow the numbers in your planning chart, measuring, counting, and labeling the warp sections as you stretch.

3. STRETCH THE WARP FOR WRAPPING. Set up an ikat board/raddle system. If your table is too short for your warp, clamp one raddle onto one table and the other onto another adjacent table or surface (as described on page 35). Pull the tables apart to create the necessary distance to supply tension.

Rather than distributing each design section in sequence across the clamped raddles in 17 individual groups, simply stack and layer the similar sections on top of each other for ease in wrapping.

There are four sections that will require a 1" (2.5 cm) ikat resist, two sections that will require a 2" (5 cm) resist, and 1 section that will require a 3" (7.5 cm) resist.

Solid stripe, dyed	Accent color	2" (5 cm) ikat resist/4" (10 cm) dyed	Accent color	Solid stripe, no dye	1" (2.5 cm) ikat resist/2" (5 cm) dyed	Solid stripe, no dye	Accent color	3" (7.5 cm) ikat resist /4" (10 cm) dyed	Accent color	Solid stripe, no dye	1" (2.5 cm) ikat resist/2" (5 cm) dyed	Solid stripe, no dye	Accent color	2" (5 cm) ikat resist/4" (10 cm) dyed	Accent color	Solid stripe, dyed
48	14	126	4	15	15	15	4	126	4	15	15	15	4	126	14	48

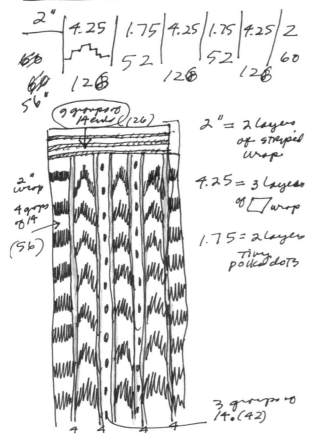

figure 1: The rough sketch.

A and M: Indigo
B, D, F, H, J, and L: Colored yarn accent
C and K: 2" (5 cm) wide wraps stacked on each other (indigo)
E and I: 1" (2.5 cm) wide checkerboard wraps stacked (indigo)
G: 4" (10 cm) wide wrap (indigo)

figure 2: The working sketch for the Mediterranean Stole.

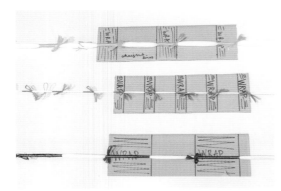

figure 3

figure 4

figure 5

4. MAKE A GUIDE FOR WRAPPING. Because the ikat-resist pattern for each of the groups of threads is simple and repetitive, a full-size cartoon isn't necessary. Instead, you'll make a wrapping guide for each group that includes several repeats of each resist pattern. The guide includes both the length to be resisted and the length to be dyed. Cut three pieces of cardboard, drawing several repeats of each of the three ikat design sections on each. Use them as your template, advancing them down the stretched warp (**figure 3**). There's no need to mark onto the warp or draw the entire design out on a big sheet of Kraft paper.

5. DYE THE WARP. This stole is dyed using indigo. Use the dye of your choice but be sure to treat the yarns that you are not dyeing in the scour bath so that shrinkage will be the same as the rest of the warp. A commercially dyed yarn is used for the weft. (***Note:*** Also treat the commercially dyed yarns.) Carefully unwrap the yarns when dyeing is complete and dry.

6. WARP THE LOOM AND SHIFT THE WARP THREADS. Lay out all of the sections in sequence and load them onto the lease sticks. Thread the warp through the reed and heddles, knotting and stabilizing your warp in small bundles of 7 ends, which, when tied together on the back beam, will become groups of 14 ends. C-clamp the wooden warp-shifting device onto the loom's back support beam.

Begin advancing bundles of 7 and tie them together onto the warp-beam rod. When you reach the center design section to be shifted, thread two groups of 7 ends through each slit in the warp-shifting device and then tie directly onto the warp-beam rod (**figures 4 and 5**). The tool causes the threads to "detour," thus shifting the ikat.

Continue to tie on the other sections that are not to be shifted, being careful to maintain the design integrity of the small ikat square and 2" (5 cm) bar. The warp-shifting tool remains secured to the back of your loom, held in place by the C-clamps, throughout the weaving process. Occasionally check to make sure your warp is feeding accurately through the device.

Alternatively, the warp threads can be shifted using staggered knots or staggered cords.

7. WEAVE. Now weave the stole and let the warp-shifting device work its magic!

After you've finished making this stole, move on to weaving the variation, Byzantine Arrows, which follows next.

BYZANTINE ARROWS

The arrangement of warps in this piece is identical to the Mediterranean Stole, except the warps on the borders use 1" (2.5 cm) ikat resists instead of a solid dye color. You'll shift the three center ikat sections using a larger warp-shifting tool with three identical shifting units. Download the cartoon for this project from www.interweave.com/IkatCartoons. Feel free to create your own palette, collating the warp sections together as you load the lease sticks. Follow the same process as for the Mediterranean Stole.

EQUIPMENT

4-shaft loom, 24" (61 cm) weaving width; 12-dent reed; 1 boat shuttle.

YARNS

WARP: 8/2 Tencel (3,360 yd/lb [7,378 m/kg]; WEBS), White for ikat, 18 oz (510 g); commercially dyed green for stripes, 2 oz (57 g).

WEFT: 60/2 Valley Yarns silk (100% silk, 15,000 yd/lb [30,028 m/kg]; WEBS), Medium Navy (#634) for borders, 2 oz (57 g).

OTHER SUPPLIES

Basic Toolkit (page 78).

WARP LENGTH

600 ends 4 yd (3.7 m) long (allows 33" for take-up, fringe, ikat adjustment, and loom waste).

SETTS

WARP: 30 epi (2/dent in a 15-dent reed).

WEFT: 20 ppi.

DIMENSIONS

WIDTH IN THE REED: 20" (51 cm).
WOVEN LENGTH: 87" (221 cm) (measured under tension on the loom).
FINISHED SIZE: 19" × 83" (48 cm × 211 cm).

NOTES

The shifting of the ikat directly relates to the depth of the slits in the warp-shifting tool (figures 1 and 2).

figure 1

figure 2

americana scarf

This two-dyebath ikat warp weaves into a scarf that looks far more complex than it actually is. The process adds a second dyepot of color and weft color changes.

IKAT SKILL

A cardboard DIY measuring and wrapping template works well as a quick and simple tool for evenly spacing the distance between the individual warp sections to be wrapped, guiding as you wrap your way down the warp. The starting point for each ikat warp bundle begins 1" (2.5 cm) up from the previous one, creating a diagonal pattern across the warp sections. This project also includes a full-sized cartoon.

STRUCTURE

Plain weave.

EQUIPMENT

4-shaft loom, 15" (38 cm) weaving width; 12-dent reed; lease sticks; 2 boat shuttles.

YARNS

WARP: 8/2 Tencel (3,360 yd/lb [7,378 m/kg]; WEBS), White, 7 oz (200 g).

WEFT: 60/2 Valley Yarns silk: Medium Navy (#634) and #618 Red (100% silk, 15,000 yd/lb [30,028 m/kg]; WEBS), Navy, 1 oz (28 g); Red #618, 1 oz (28 g).

DYES

Procion MX fiber reactive dyes

• Blue: Indigo #422N

• Red: Mixing Red #305 + Strongest Red #312N + Turkey Red #320

OTHER SUPPLIES

Basic Toolkit (page 78); cardboard for ikat tying guide, 2 × 14" (5 × 35.5 cm); 1 set of raddles or ikat boards; 4 C-clamps, 3" (7.5 cm); ikat tape or other resist-wrapping materials.

WARP LENGTH

312 ends 3 yd (2.7 m) long (allows 34" [86 cm] for take-up, fringe, ikat adjustment, and loom waste).

SETTS

WARP: 24 epi (2/dent in a 12-dent reed).
WEFT: 28 ppi.

DIMENSIONS

WIDTH IN THE REED: 13½" (34 cm).
WOVEN LENGTH: 71½" (182 cm) (measured under tension on the loom).
FINISHED SIZE: 70" × 12" (178 cm × 30 cm).

PROCESS

1. DESIGN THE WARPING AND WRAPPING PLAN. You can either download, print, and assemble the cartoon I created for this project from www.interweave.com/IkatCartoons, or just use the ikat cardboard measuring and wrapping template as described below.

The warp for the Americana Scarf is wound as (13) 1" (2.5 cm) individual sections. The design plan calls for the 13 warp-stripe sections to be wrapped in an ascending pattern, using the cardboard ikat measuring template. Stretch each of the warp sections between the two ikat boards or raddles. To create the proper tension for wrapping, this warp requires weights at one end **(figure 1)**.

Label and number each warp section consecutively, 1 to 13. Place them in order between your ikat boards.

Beginning with the first section, and using the cardboard template as a guide, bind off 3" (7.5 cm), and leave 4" (10 cm) unbound for dye. Move the cardboard up the length of that warp section, wrapping the repetitive pattern.

When you get to the end of the first section, move to section #2 but begin the binding sequence 1" (2.5 cm) up from where the first one started. Complete the binding for warp section #2. Continue in this way, moving from section 1 to 13, always beginning 1" (2.5 cm) up when beginning a new warp section. The 1" (2.5 cm) advance of each section causes the ascending pattern of the ikat **(figure 2)**.

When all the wrapping is complete, divide the warp bundles into two groups: even-numbered and odd-numbered sections.

2. DYE. Only the warp is dyed. The odd-numbered groups will be dyed blue. The even-numbered groups will be dyed red. Follow Procion MX fiber reactive dye instructions or use natural dyes if you prefer. Carefully remove the wrapping and dry the yarn.

3. WARP. Place the unwrapped dyed warp sections on a table in numerical order. If you followed the plan, each warp stripe should be of a different alternating color, forming an ascending geometric design.

Load the sections onto your lease sticks and warp your loom **(figure 3)**. Tie the individual bundles onto the warp-beam rod, making sure to tweak and position each bundle to create the "ascending" look.

What additional kinds of creative magic can you make happen as you warp the loom with this palette of ikat sections?

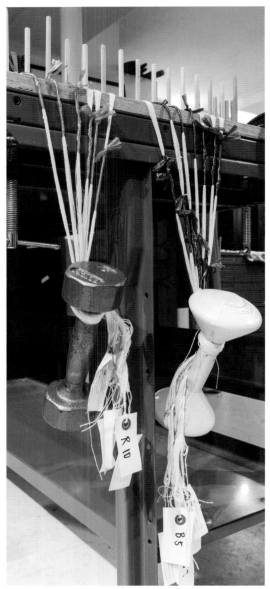

figure 1

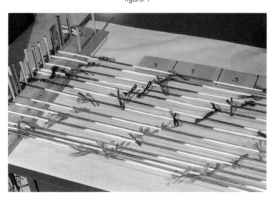

figure 2

▸ Pull the threads and create ikat-shifted patterns within each 1" (2.5 cm) bundle.

▸ Lay in warp stripes of a third color between sections.

▸ Lay in warp stripes of a variety of different colors between each ascending design section.

figure 3

4. WEAVE. Weave alternating weft blocks of blue and red weft, in the following sequence, or your own version of weft stripes (**figure 4**).

blue: 4" (10 cm)
red: 3" (7.5 cm)
blue: 5" (12.5 cm)
red: 2" (5 cm)
blue: 4" (10 cm)
red: 1" (2.5 cm)
blue: 3" (7.5 cm)
red: 2" (5 cm)
blue: 4" (10 cm)
red: 3" (7.5 cm)
blue: 5" (12.5 cm)
red: 2" (5 cm)
blue: 4" (10 cm)
red: 1" (2.5 cm)
blue: 3" (7.5 cm)
red: 2" (5 cm)
blue: 4" (10 cm)
red: 3" (7.5 cm)
blue: 5" (12.5 cm)
red: 2" (5 cm)
blue: 4" (10 cm)
red: 1" (2.5 cm)
blue: 3" (7.5 cm).

figure 4

After you've finished this scarf, tackle its variation, the Summer Scarf.

VARIATION

SUMMER SCARF

The fresh, sunny Summer Scarf is a sister to the Americana Scarf, dyed in yellow and blue. You could weave versions of these scarves forever. They're colorful and fun, offering endless possibilities, permutations, and combinations of colors, geometric patterns, and weave structures to explore. You'll find the cartoon at www.interweave.com/IkatCartoons; download, print, and assemble it. Use the same yarns and follow the same process as for the Americana Scarf.

DYES

Procion MX fiber reactive dyes on warp

• Yellow: Golden Yellow #104 + Clear Yellow #1229

• Blue: Basic Blue #400 + Mixing Blue #402c

Procion MX fiber reactive dyes on weft

• Yellow: Golden Yellow #104 + Clear Yellow #1229

NOTES

This version has four additional warp threads of a third color, red, added to each selvedge as a small border. The red warps are commercially dyed yarns. The scarf is woven with a solid-colored yellow weft.

The individual yellow and blue ikat warp bundles are organized on the lease sticks in a random staggered pattern prior to weaving **(figure 1)**. Three ½" (1.3 cm) blue weft stripes were added at each end for contrast. The materials, weave structure, setts, and dimensions are the same as the Americana Scarf.

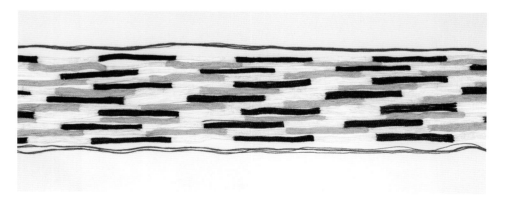

figure 1

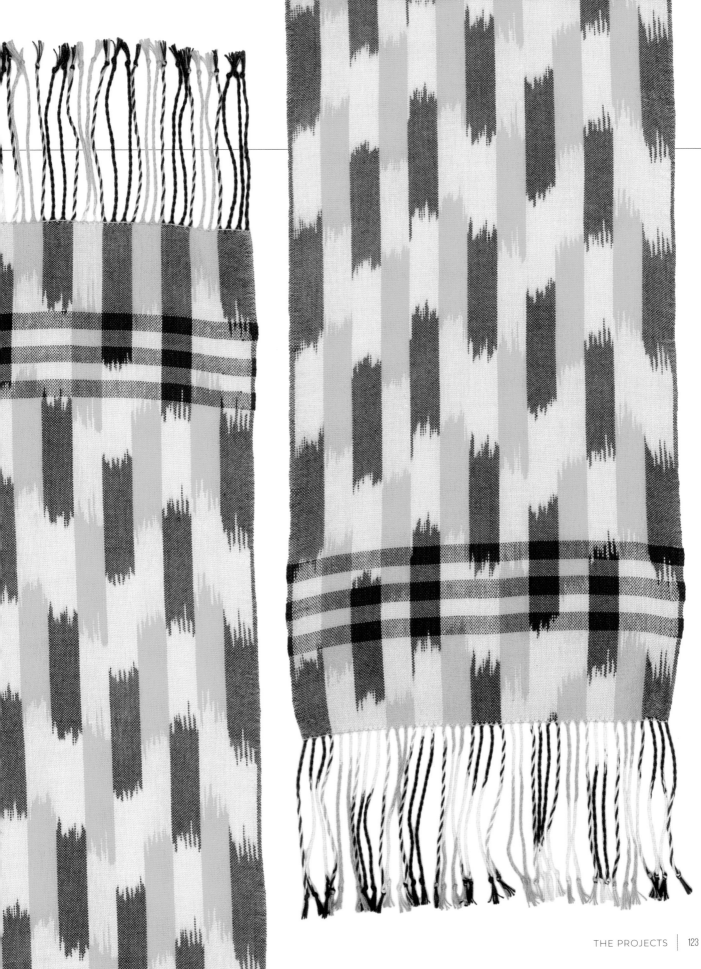

peruvian runner

The design for the Peruvian Runner was inspired by a Step Design Mantle from the Nasca culture of Peru, which experts believe was woven between 200 and 600 CE. It's a simple three-color block pattern, an excellent composition for introducing multiple dyed colors on a warp.

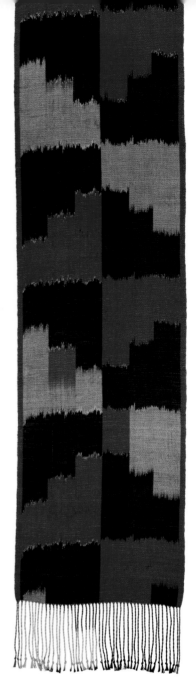

IKAT SKILL

This is the first project that isn't a simple one-step ikat resist that preserves the original white yarns. The warps are wrapped and dyed, then unwrapped, rewrapped in a different area, and dyed again. This makes overdyeing possible, as well as showcasing multiple blocks of wrapped and dyed colors.

STRUCTURE

Plain weave.

EQUIPMENT

4-shaft loom, 24" (61 cm) weaving width; 12-dent reed; lease sticks; 1 boat shuttle.

YARNS

WARP: 20/2 Normandy Linen, (wet-spun line linen, 3,000 yd/lb [6,038 m/kg]; Yarn Barn of Kansas), Bleached Ivory, 8 oz (228 g).

WEFT: 20/2 silk (5,000 yd/lb [10,800 m/kg]; Georgia Yarn Company), 2 oz (57 g), left over from a previous project.

DYES

Procion MX fiber reactive dyes for linen warp

• Dyebath #1 Blue: Navy #412 + Indigo #422N

• Dyebath #2 Red: Basic Red #310N + Turkey Red #320

• Dyebath #3 Yellow: Golden Yellow #104 + Clear Yellow #1229

Indigo vat for silk weft

OTHER SUPPLIES

Basic Toolkit (page 78); Kraft paper 80 × 14½" (203 × 37 cm), optional; 1 set of raddles or stretching boards; 4 C-clamps, 3" (7.5 cm); ikat tape or other resist-wrapping material.

WARP LENGTH

288 ikat ends + borders, 3 yd (2.7 m) long (allows 34" (86 cm) for take-up, fringe, ikat adjustment, and loom waste).

SETTS

WARP: 24 epi (2/dent in a 12-dent reed).
WEFT: 20 ppi.

DIMENSIONS

WIDTH IN THE REED: 16½–19½" (42–50 cm).
WOVEN LENGTH: 82" (208 cm) (measured under tension on the loom).
FINISHED SIZE: 80" × 14½" (203 cm × 37 cm).

NOTES

This project gets fancy. The only way you can totally capture the look of a three-dyepot overdyed warp ikat is to stretch, wrap, dye, unwrap, restretch, rewrap, and dye three times. These additional steps are not more difficult, only more involved. If you've been making the projects sequentially as presented in the book, you're ready for it—you've got the basics under your belt!

This Nasca Stepped Mantle, woven in Peru between 200–600 CE, is the inspiration for the author's design. Image courtesy of William Siegal Gallery, Santa Fe, NM.

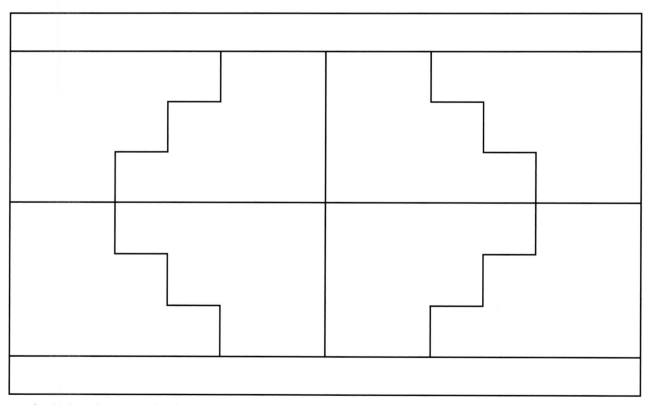

Based on the mantle shown at top, the author created this section of design, then repeated it four times lengthwise on a much larger sheet of paper to create the full cartoon.

PROCESS

1. CREATE THE CARTOON. Download, print, and assemble my cartoon for this project at www.interweave.com/IkatCartoons, or draw your own. If you create your own, refer to the original image to draw it at the finished size on Kraft paper, enlarging it and drawing it to scale. Is your drawing balanced? Do you like it? If not, tweak and rethink the proportions, creating a design that pleases you. Label all of the sections, indicating the color they'll be dyed. This will be the official wrapping guide.

2. WIND THE WARP. In order to reproduce my cartoon, you'll need six bundles of warp (48 threads each). Wind them all on the warping board at the same time but tie each warp bundle off separately. Wind two borders 12 to 36 threads each; the width of the border is your design decision.

Do not cut the ends; leave in the loops and tie both ends of each warp bundle together into a single loop with a thick piece of yarn (**figure 1**).

Bag both ends of each warp bundle together and bind for an inch or two (2.5–5 cm) with ikat tape (page 43) to prepare for scouring. Bagging the ends of the warp sections will protect them from getting snarled and jumbled. The ends will ultimately be loom waste so you don't need to scour and dye them.

If your project involves multiple dyebaths, pre-scour the entire warp (less the bagged ends) before any wrapping occurs. This reduces wear and tear on the fiber and helps preserve the quality of the color. Bagging the ends will keep the end loops protected and free from tangling with each other during the scouring (**figure 2**). It only takes a few minutes to do and ultimately saves steps and lots of time.

Set up a pair of stretching/raddle boards on your work surface. Tape the cartoon on the table between the boards, taking into account the number of inches/cm you planned for fringe and loom waste. You have approximately 1 yard (91.5 cm) to play with, so adjust the cartoon to suit.

Unbag the scoured warp and place the warp bundles in order. Loop each uncut warp bundle through a dowel on one end. Place the warp-carrying dowel behind the pegs of one of the ikat stretching boards or raddle. Loop the other ends through another dowel and place that behind the pegs on the other stretching board.

Now gently pull the ends away from each other, providing a bit of tension to the warp as you divide and distribute the warp sections to match your cartoon. Adjust the cartoon and warp as needed. The width of the cartoon will seem odd, much wider than the skinny sections of warp. This is not a mistake. It is to scale. The thin bundles of warp will transform and expand to be the correct width after dressing the loom and weaving. The cartoon provides the critical starting and stopping information for wrapping and is the road map for dyeing.

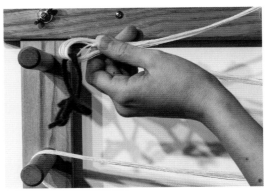

figure 1

figure 2

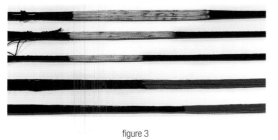

figure 3

3. WRAP AND DYE. With your warp organized and in place, you're ready to begin the wrapping and dyeing sequence. But first, note that the repeated wrapping, unwrapping, stretching, restretching, and dyeing that you're about to undertake will ask a lot of your 600 warp threads. Things can happen to the fibers en route. The wraps may loosen and can sometimes come off. Dye could inadvertently wick up under the most carefully wrapped tape. Colors might mix and blend (**figure 3**), creating unexpected surprises. Check your wraps at every step, but this is the nature of ikat—embrace it!

What happens in an ikat dyepot stays in an ikat dyepot, and is often impossible to replicate exactly. This is both the blessing and the curse of resist-dyeing methods. A white undyed halo could surround your dyed color blocks (**figure 4**); to avoid this overlap your wrap a tiny bit onto the previous color. If you want more surprises, and more wicking and bleed in the dyepot, simply loosen, puncture, or randomly remove wraps. If you want more control, double-check wrapped areas and reinforce the taped areas that look weary. Handle the yarn gently when dyeing, and then chant, pray, and make oblations to the ikat gods.

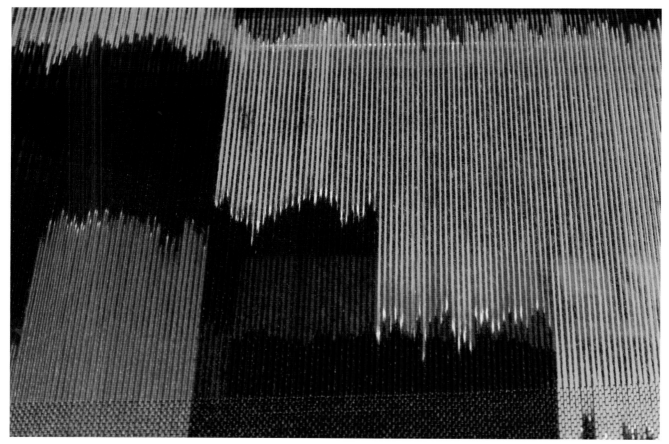

figure 4

Wrap and dye as follows:

▶ **BLUE:** Cover and wrap the warp in the design areas designated red and yellow. Those are *not* going to be dyed blue. That leaves 15 sections of unwrapped exposed white warp that will be dyed blue (**figure 5**). Lift the warp off the boards. You can re-bag the end loops at this point to protect them. Wet out the yarns and dye the warp bundles in a blue dyebath. Rinse. You can allow the yarn to dry after dyeing or move on to the next step while it's wet.

▶ **RED:** Carefully untangle the dyed warp and restretch it between the boards. Unwrap the areas that are to be dyed red; this is eight design sections (**figure 6**). Protect and wrap all of the blue. *Do not unwrap the areas you've already wrapped; they will be dyed yellow in the next step.* Lift and remove the warp from the boards. Bag your ends if you wish; wet out the warp bundles and dye them in a red dyepot, along with the border warp sections. Rinse.

▶ **YELLOW:** Carefully untangle the dyed warp and once again restretch between the boards. Unwrap the sections to be dyed yellow. Don't touch the blue wrapped areas; leave them wrapped (**figure 7**) and re-bag your ends. Put the warp into the yellow dyepot with resist-wrapping left on *only* the blue sections. The exposed red yarn will be overdyed with yellow and the freshly unwrapped white yarn will also be dyed yellow. The border sections can be overdyed with yellow if you choose. Rinse the yarns.

After the final dyebath, unwrap all the remaining resists (**figure 8**). The final step is to boil out the excess dye. All the warp bundles can be boiled together as the dye has been set and the colors won't bleed. Refer to the fiber reactive dye directions (page 66, step 7) if you need to refresh your memory.

4. WARP AND WEAVE. You've now completed the heavy lifting on this project, successfully preparing a three-dyebath warp ikat. You're ready to weave. The rest is a breeze.

As with the previous warp projects, how you handle the warp yarns as you dress the loom will affect the amount of design shifting. If you want big solid red, yellow, and blue color blocks with little feathering, you'll need to carefully control the warp bundles. As I've previously mentioned, this process of trying to control dyed ikat threads, keeping them lined up, organized, and arranged in some sense of pleasing order, is referred to as "fussing."

After you're warped and tied on, select the weft weight and color. The sample runner shown on these pages was woven with a mid-range 20/2 indigo-dyed silk left over from earlier projects. In my studio, we dyed many silk hanks so we'd have a supply of indigo weft yarns on hand; you might consider doing the same with each dyebath color. This hank came out of the indigo vat rather unevenly dyed, which actually worked out surprisingly well when put in combination with the multicolored warp.

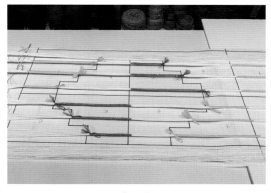

figure 5

figure 6

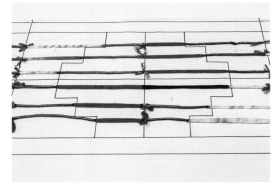

figure 7

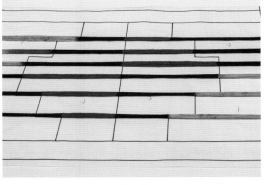

figure 8

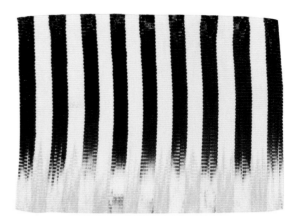

seaside placemats

This project introduces weft ikat through the simple repetitive format of the placemat. Seventeen classic alternating stripes are the only design element. Cotton bamboo, a thick absorbent yarn, is a suitable choice for the resist-dyed weft, the agent for the ikat magic. I dyed two colorways of this design, so you'll see examples of both in these instructions. This project is weft-ikat boot camp—roll up your sleeves because there's a lot to learn!

IKAT SKILL

This project introduces weft ikat. You'll learn how to wind weft yarns and dye them for ikat resist.

STRUCTURE

Plain weave.

EQUIPMENT

4-shaft loom, 17" (43 cm) weaving width; 8-dent reed; 2 stick shuttles.

YARNS

WARP: 22/2 Bockens Cottolin (3,200 yd/lb [6390 m/kg]; Yarn Barn of Kansas), White, 4 oz (114 g).

WEFT: Bamboo Cotton (51% combed organic cotton/49% rayon from bamboo, 990 yd/lb [1820 m/kg; Ravel, Henry's Attic), 8 oz (225 g).

DYES

Procion MX fiber reactive dyes

• Black: Black #628

• Willow: Chartreuse #706

• Blue: MX Indigo #422N

Dye materials and auxiliaries.

OTHER SUPPLIES

Basic Toolkit (page 78); 1 set of raddles or stretching boards; 4 C-clamps, 3" (7.5 cm); ikat tape or other resist-wrapping material, plastic freezer bags.

WARP LENGTH

112 ends, 4 yd (3.7 m) long (allows for 4 placemats with 76" [193 cm] for take-up, fringe, and loom waste).

SETTS

WARP: 8 epi (1/dent in an 8-dent reed).
WEFT: 28 ppi.

DIMENSIONS

WIDTH IN THE REED: 14" (36 cm).
WOVEN LENGTH: 17¼" (44 cm) per placemat (measured under tension on the loom).
FINISHED SIZE: 17" × 13" (43 cm × 33 cm).

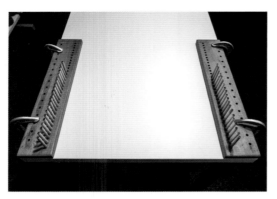

figure 1

PROCESS

1. WARP THE LOOM. In this project, unlike the others, the warp won't act as the virtuoso. It will be totally hidden from view in the weft-face weave; its job is simply to provide structural support, like the studs of a house, for the yarns carrying the ikat. Refer to the yarns and setts. Gather materials. Measure the warp, 116 ends at 6 yd (5.5 m) long. Warp the loom.

2. PREPARE TO MEASURE THE WEFT. Establish and set the peg-to-peg distance between the two stretching boards approximately ½" (13 mm) wider than the desired width of your placemat. Clamp the boards to the work surface, making sure they're squared, not skewed or clamped at an angle. You want precisely the same distance—measure it! —between pegs at each end. You'll stretch the entire weft for one set of four placemats between the pegs on the stretching boards (**figure 1**).

3. PLAN THE DESIGN. The finished length of each placemat is 17" (43 cm), composed of (17) 1" (2.5 cm) stripes. Nine of the stripes will be wrapped and dyed in a black dyebath. You'll wind and dye the weft for all the black stripes together. The remaining eight stripes will be wrapped in a different sequence and dyed in a willow green dyebath.

4. CALCULATE THE WEFT PICKS. To move forward with weft calculations, you need to know the number of picks per inch (ppi) at which the yarn is going to weave. The yarn that I used wove at 28 ppi (11 picks per cm).

If you're using a different yarn, you'll need to calculate the number of picks per inch or cm. Wrap a length of the yarn around a ruler and count the number of comfortably spaced wraps per inch. This number of wraps is your picks per inch or cm.

Armed with this information, one plan might be to wrap 28 picks (14 revolutions) of the weft yarn back and forth between one set of opposing pegs on your ikat boards. The pegs will hold that much yarn. However, a thick fat yarn like this, when wrapped and dyed, will create a chunky look when woven. Instead, distribute the 28 picks (14 revolutions) between two sets of pegs for a more lyrical woven ikat line.

To create the more lyrical feathered ikat "line," wind seven revolutions on each peg, then move to the next peg. The 28 picks (14 revolutions) will be distributed between two sets of pegs.

The design plan calls for nine stripes wound on 18 pegs to be wrapped and dyed black. Eight stripes are wound on 16 pegs to be wrapped and dyed willow green, with each peg carrying seven revolutions (14 picks) of stretched yarn.

GETTING STRETCHING BOARDS SQUARE

It's very important in weft ikat that the stretching boards be set up squarely and securely. Even as small as a ⅛" (3 mm) discrepancy in width measurement between the top and the bottom of the boards can cause the weaving to become a frustrating mishmash of a mess. Here's a trick to get it right (follow along with **figure a**).

1. Line up a first board flush with the end of the worktable, creating a justified edge. Clamp both the top and bottom.

2. Measure the peg-to-peg distance, adding extra width, and C-clamp the second board to the table.

In most situations you'll only have access to one edge of the table to C-clamp the second board to. So what do you do to prevent the unsecured end of the board from pulling in as you stretch row after row of tensioned weft between the pegs? In my studio, for most projects we use blocks of wood scraps that we call jigs. We keep a box of various lengths, placing them in various configurations next to each other at the top, between the boards, set at the same exact width as the bottom. This keeps the boards exactly parallel to each other and doesn't interfere with yarn stretching or wrapping.

Another solution is to cut a piece of plywood the exact length of your two boards/raddles to use as a faux tabletop, allowing access to all sides for clamping. For extremely wide wefts of 5 feet (1.5 m) or more, secure the boards with screws directly onto a piece of plywood to ensure that each stretched row is precisely the same as the last.

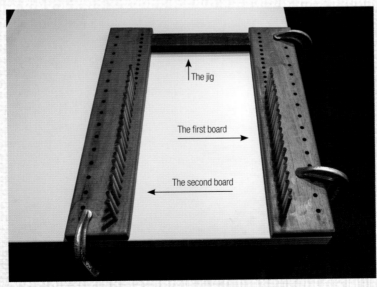

figure a

figure 2

figure 3

figure 4

figure 5

5. WIND THE WEFT. Begin winding your weft yarn for the first color in the lower left-hand corner, attaching it to the bottom left peg (aka peg #1–left) of the board. With even tension, stretch the weft across to the corresponding peg on the opposite board, rounding the peg (peg #1–right) and then returning back to where you started. This represents one revolution and two woven picks. Do this for a total of 7 revolutions. After revolution 7, after rounding the bottom left peg, stretch the yarn across the distance between the boards and now move up and around the next peg (peg #2–right), returning back to the partner peg on the matching board (peg #2–left) rather than returning to the original bottom peg #1 (**figure 2**). This begins a new peg and counting sequence of 7 revolutions. Move up the board every 7 wrapping revolutions to a new peg until you've loaded a total of 18 pegs. Perform this with a continuous length of yarn stretched under consistent even tension.

To keep the yarn and design sequence organized, twine both sides of the stretched yarns while they're on the ikat boards. Don't use your weft yarn; instead, use a slippery firm thread such as a length of linen or cotton rug warp. Twine over and under each section of the stretched yarn (**figure 3**) and return back to the start, securing the ends without pulling taut (**figure 4** shows how this will look). This completes the weft winding for one set of stripes for the first placemat.

In order that all four placemats look identical, with the ikat design falling in exactly the same place on each mat, repeat the sequence, winding the weft and stacking 4 layers on top of each other. Place a piece of paper between each stretched layer of threads. This allows the section to be twined without inadvertently picking up the threads from the previous layer. Figure 5 shows this in action; 2 layers have been wound, there's a sheet of paper on top of the 2nd layer, and winding has just begun for a 3rd layer. Remove the protective sheets of paper placed between each layer of weft prior to wrapping the ikat.

6. WRAP THE WEFT. Once the twining has been completed for each layer, remove the paper separators. The simplest method to guide your wrapping for these mats is to place a piece of masking tape down on the table beneath the stretched weft, approximately 3–4" (7.5–10 cm) from one looped edge. Use the tape as your guide and wrap several inches into the resisted area of the weft (**figure 6**, page 136). There's no need to wrap all the way to the end. You'll eventually encounter the "opposite peg dilemma." How do you wrap and cover a length of yarn stretched between pegs or nails when a peg is in the way and you want the end of the yarn hank to be wrapped and protected from dye?

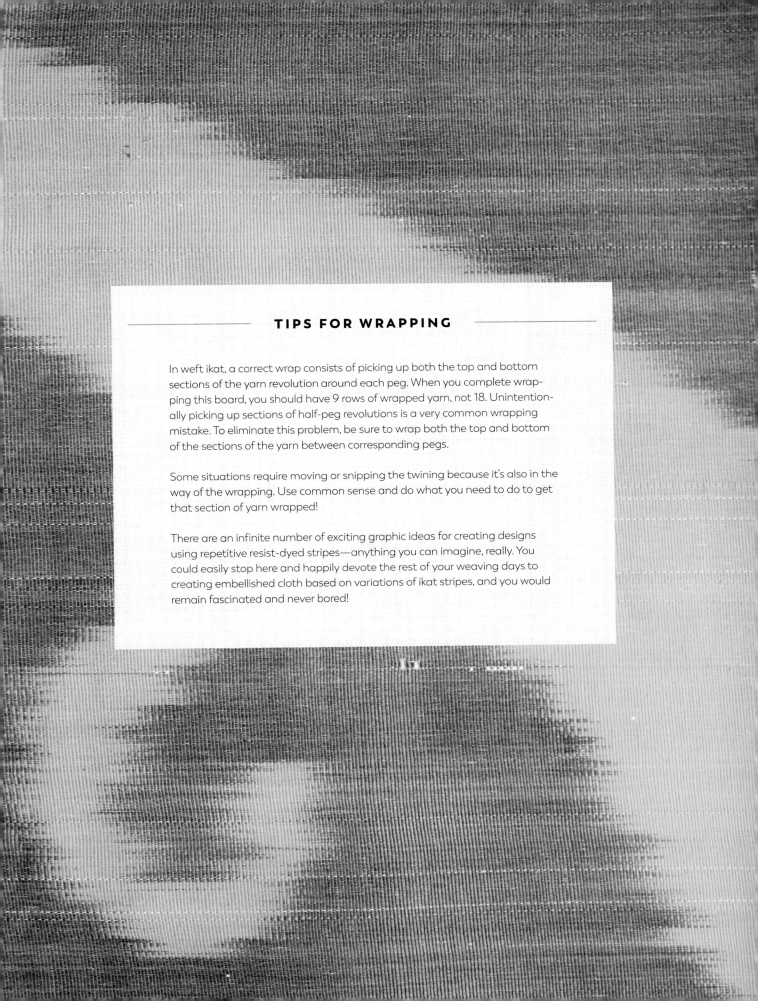

TIPS FOR WRAPPING

In weft ikat, a correct wrap consists of picking up both the top and bottom sections of the yarn revolution around each peg. When you complete wrapping this board, you should have 9 rows of wrapped yarn, not 18. Unintentionally picking up sections of half-peg revolutions is a very common wrapping mistake. To eliminate this problem, be sure to wrap both the top and bottom of the sections of the yarn between corresponding pegs.

Some situations require moving or snipping the twining because it's also in the way of the wrapping. Use common sense and do what you need to do to get that section of yarn wrapped!

There are an infinite number of exciting graphic ideas for creating designs using repetitive resist-dyed stripes—anything you can imagine, really. You could easily stop here and happily devote the rest of your weaving days to creating embellished cloth based on variations of ikat stripes, and you would remain fascinated and never bored!

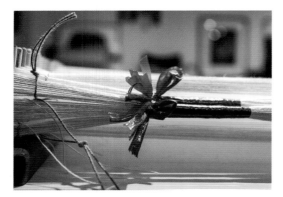

figure 6

figure 7

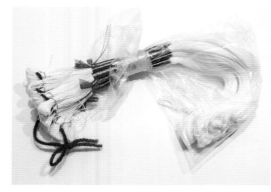

figure 8

Wrap each section up to and as close to the pegs as is comfortable. Lift the wrapped sections from the pegs and then continue wrapping them together for a bit, now as one unit. Bag your ends by placing the unwrapped end sections in a plastic freezer bag, securing tightly with ikat tape. Double-bag the ends (**figure 7**).

7. BUNDLE AND BAG THE WRAPPED WEFT. Bundle and wrap all four sections of each design area at one time. As you take the weft off of the boards, remove the yarn loops off of the pegs and thread a thick piece of yarn through each loop, as if you were threading beads on a necklace. Tie the ends together to form a big yarn loop (**figure 8**). This is an important step because it will help keep the yarns organized in the dyepot. All four layers are now stretched, wrapped, and connected, and they will all go into the same dyepot together in step 8.

After you've completed wrapping the yarns for the black stripes, repeat steps 5 and 6 for the willow stripes, but wind only 8 stripes, or 16 pegs of weft. Begin the wrapping from the other side of the masking tape guide, and use the chart below as a guide.

8. DYE THE WEFT. Dyeing weft ikat doesn't require a different dye system than warp ikat. But you'll notice a difference because of the volume of yarn. You're no longer dealing with long lengths of warp that want to tangle in the dyepot. The issue now is short compressed sections that bunch together, making it harder for the dye to penetrate.

For this project you've stretched and wrapped two distinctly different sections of weft yarns, each to be dyed in a different colored dyebath. Remember to weigh each section before scouring in order to accurately calculate your weight of fiber—WOF—when dyeing. For efficiency, scour the weft sections together. Pin the bagged end bundles with a clothespin up above the liquid in the dyepot. Wrapped yarns love to wick dye.

After dyeing, remove the thick piece of yarn threaded through the loops and carefully pull the twined layers apart. Hang the weft to dry.

9. LOAD THE SHUTTLES. When the weft is dry, lay out the yarn sections in the order they'll be woven. A tip for smoothly loading your shuttles is to reload the ikat boards with the weft yarns. The yarn groups don't have to be neatly and perfectly loaded as for wrapping ikat. The job of the boards is to now just provide some organization and enough tension so the weft yarn can be wound on shuttles. Load your shuttles backwards, from top to bottom of the yarn-design section, so the first shot you weave is the first shot you stretched.

WILLOW DYE: 4" (10 cm)	WRAPPED RESIST: 10" (26 cm)
WRAPPED RESIST: 4" (10 cm)	BLACK DYE: 10" (26 cm)

figure 9

figure 10

10. WEAVE THE WEFT. Weave in your header. Lay several rows of the weft yarn on top of the warp to determine whether the ikat design lays in on itself and "fits" (**figure 9**). The amount of bubbling you do will affect the fit, as will where you begin to lay in the first shot of weaving. It takes three shots of weaving to determine whether your weft yarns fit your warp. Don't absentmindedly throw the shuttle; the weaving requires focus. Each shot requires lining up the design, then adjusting the tension and bubbling to accommodate the design, particularly at the beginning (**figure 10**). As I mentioned before, this is referred to as *fussing*.

Continue to line up and adjust your weft with each shot that you weave. If your weft pattern suddenly falls out of alignment, it can be corrected. The cause is usually inconsistent tension when stretching the weft on the ikat board or inconsistent tension and bubbling when weaving. You can't do anything to change what happened at the ikat boards, but you can adjust your weaving. Take out the culprit shot and lay it in differently. If that doesn't work, create a tuck in the weft by forming a loop to take up slack and realign the ikat. Continue on to your next shot. Snip the ends of the loop and weave them into the woven cloth in a warp-wise direction (**figure 11**).

TIP: To create weft ikat with "guaranteed" justified selvedges, warp the loom a little wider than your project dimensions, adding a few more warp threads than you think you'll need. To make an ikat-weft pattern fit and weave beautifully with clean selvedges, adjust your warp to fit the weft, rather than vice versa. Simply drop off or eliminate a warp end or two or three, or add on a few. This allows the ikat to rule.

Because the weft of the Seaside Placemats is a dense weft-face weave, it allows for the many weft ends created by the color-changing stripes to be woven back up into the cloth, tails trimmed and buried, rather than overlapped during weaving (**figures 12–15**).

11. FINISHING. The warp threads can be woven back into the cloth for a clean finish or, if you prefer, begin and end each placemat with three shots to 1 woven inch (2.5 woven cm) of the 22/2 cottolin warp. This will stabilize and firmly secure the woven mat, allowing you to fringe the warp or give you a nice option for turning a hem.

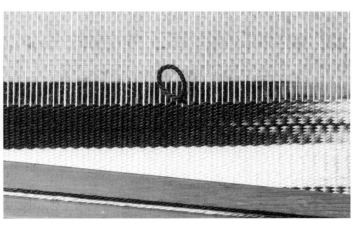

figure 11

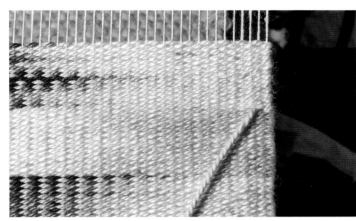

figure 12

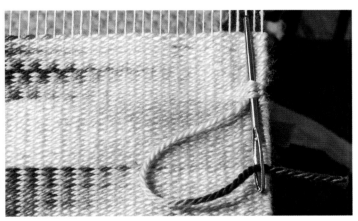

figure 13

figure 14

figure 15

cross+fire scarf

The charisma and challenge of double ikat is the clever and beautiful intersection of patterned yarns, both warp and weft, matched up during the weaving process. Throughout this book, you've seen photos showing a variety of examples of double ikats created by master weavers. This simplified project aims to demystify the art of the intersection of ikat warp with ikat weft. You already own the skill set required for double ikat. You know how to calculate, wind, wrap, and dye. Now you'll put both skill sets to work simultaneously. Go ahead, get bold and complex. Run with it!

IKAT SKILL

You'll combine a simple warp ikat with a simple weft ikat. The goal is to create purposeful and accurate warp and weft intersection. The result is a double ikat.

STRUCTURE

Plain weave.

EQUIPMENT

4-shaft loom, 17" (43 cm) weaving width; 15-dent reed; lease sticks; 1 boat shuttle.

YARNS

WARP: 20/2 Valley Yarns Tencel (8,400 yd/lb [16,950 m/kg]; WEBS), Natural, 3 oz (85 g).

WEFT:
• 50/2 silk (11,000 yd/lb [22,000 m/kg]; Henry's Attic, Yarn Barn of Kansas), 2 oz (57 g).
• Gold Rush (80% rayon/20% metalized polyester, 109 yd/0.87 oz [99.6 m/0.025 kg]; Lincatex, Yarn Barn of Kansas), Copper, 13 yd.

DYES

WARP AND WEFT: Procion MX fiber reactive dye, Black #628

OTHER SUPPLIES

Basic Toolkit (page 78); Kraft paper, 11 × 72" (28 × 183 cm); 1 set of raddles or stretching boards; 4 C-clamps, 3" (7.5 cm); ikat tape or other resist-wrapping material.

WARP LENGTH

330 ends, 3¼ yd (3 m) long (allows 32" [81 cm] for take-up, ikat shifting, fringe, and loom waste).

SETTS

WARP: 30 epi (2/dent in a 15-dent reed).
WEFT: 40 ppi.

DIMENSIONS

WIDTH IN THE REED: 11" (28 cm).
WOVEN LENGTH: 91" (231 cm) (measured under tension on the loom).
FINISHED SIZE: 10¼" × 88" (26 cm × 224 cm).

NOTES

At the last minute I added four warps of copper metallic thread to each selvedge to add bling, in hopes of enhancing the wine color. I was fully aware that adding eight threads would change the width of my warp and have an impact on matching up my ikat-weft design. To compensate, I removed four black threads from each side.

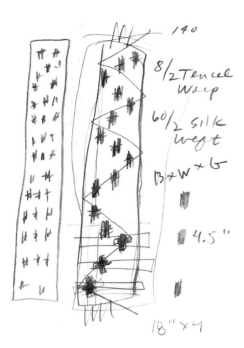

figure 1: The rough sketch.

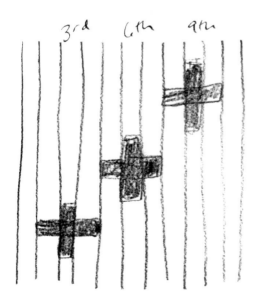

figure 2: The rough sketch refined.

1. PLAN THE DESIGN. You can print and assemble the template for my design, which is online at interweave.com/IkatCartoons. If you prefer to create your own design, begin by drawing a very simple rough sketch to guide your planning. My rough sketch is shown in figure 1; in figure 2, you can see how I refined the single motif. In figure 3 it was enlarged to full size and graphed. Finally, it was made into a full-size cartoon on Kraft paper by repeating the motif section 4 times. The repeating motif section is critical to helping you to organize the weft.

2. PLAN THE WARP. The cartoon is the approximate size of the finished scarf—11 × 72" (28 × 183 cm)—and will be used as a guide for wrapping the warp yarns. Plot out the warp in (11) 1" (2.5 cm) individual sections, shading in the vertical areas of the cross representing the areas of the warp that will be resist-wrapped. Since the Tencel warp will be wound at 30 epi's, each 1" (2.5 cm) wide section of warp will consist of 30 warp threads.

3. PLAN THE WEFT. Now sketch the weft intersections on the cartoon. The cartoon is a visual guide for accurately stretching and wrapping the weft threads. Select your weft thread and calculate the number of picks per woven inch of your fiber. (This is explained in more detail in the Seaside Placemats, under Calculate the Weft Picks, page 132.) The Cross+Fire Scarf was woven with a 50/2 silk weft at 40 ppi. This weft calculation is critical as it tells you exactly how many shots of weaving will be required to create 1 woven inch (2.5 woven cm) of weft-ikat design.

Note: At 40 ppi, a 72" (183 cm) scarf will require a total number of 2,880 shots of weft. For weft intersections to match the warp at 1" (2.5 cm) in woven length, 40 strands of weft will be required to weave 1" (2.5 cm). Note that the weft will compress dramatically when woven, unlike the warp. The thin wrapped weft bundles will literally look like they could never turn into this scarf when stretched on your ikat boards. Don't panic! Just wrap them to match the weft intersections on your cartoon.

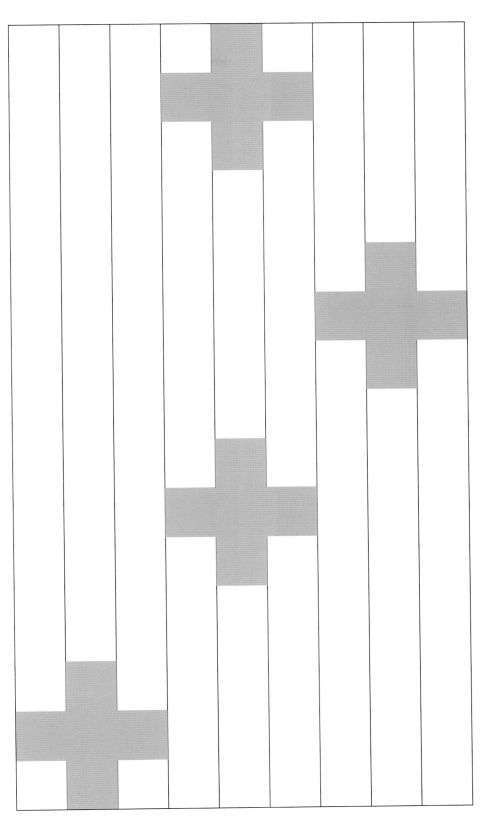

figure 3: The author enlarged a section of the rough sketch to create this section of cartoon,
which was then used as a guide to wind 4 layers of weft.

4. MEASURE, STRETCH, AND WRAP THE WARP. Measure a 330-end 3¼ yd (3 m) warp. For efficiency in organizing and wrapping, measure and divide the warp in eleven sections of 30-warp ends. Remove the 11 sections of warp, then distribute and stretch them taut between 11 pegs on 2 raddles/ ikat boards. Secure the cartoon lengthwise between the boards, beneath the stretched warp (**figure 4**). Using the cartoon as a guide, you are now ready to wrap the vertical sections of each cross motif with ikat tape.

5. STRETCH AND WRAP THE WEFT. Set up your ikat boards to be slightly wider by ¼" (6 mm) than the 11" (28 cm) planned width of the scarf. Measure the 11¼" (28.5 cm) distance from peg to peg, not from the outer edge of one board to the outer edge of the other. Secure the cartoon between the boards (**figure 5**).

Having done the math for this project, we know that 40 strands/picks (20 revolutions) of weft will equal one woven inch (2.5 woven cm).

Over the 72" (183 cm) length of the cartoon and scarf there are 4 repeats made up of 4 cross motifs. Each repeat is 18" (46 cm) long. Only 1 repeat needs to be used when binding the weft. Stretch the weft evenly for 1 repeat over 18 pegs only, loading 40 picks (or 20 full revolutions) between each pair of pegs. This will compress your design, but you can still use your cartoon as a guide for the ikat wrapping, advancing the paper if necessary. You'll stack the weft for the other 3 motif sections on top of the first.

Twine each layer separately, placing a sheet of paper on top of each layer after twining to maintain separation between the multiple layers of stretched weft. The 4 layers will be gathered up and wrapped as 1 design unit.

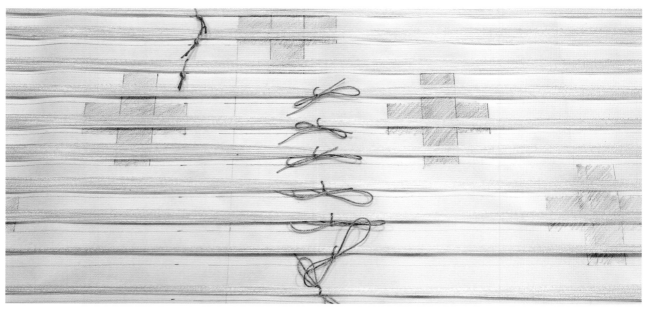

figure 4

(For those of you using the metric system, calculate as follows:

total distance ÷ 4 = x

then x ÷ 2.5 = y. [2.5 is the distance between pegs]

y = the number of pegs to distribute onto.

For example: 183 ÷ 4 = 45.8 cm, then 45.8 divided by 2.5—the distance between pegs—equals 18.)

Winding the weft will take some time as there are hundreds of shots of threads to be stretched between many pegs in several layers. Be careful to keep consistent tension. If you bear down on the fiber, pulling it extremely taut, and then loosen the tension midway in your stretching, the design won't accurately "fit" when you weave it in. Each step of preparing threads for an ikat requires consistency, mindfulness, and attention to detail.

Remember to label each board of wound and wrapped weft in proper sequence:

> ‣ Board 1, bottom left; Board 1, top right; Board 2, bottom left;
> Board 2, top right; Board 3, bottom left; Board 3, top right; etc.

These markings will help you keep your weft in proper order.

6. DYE. Weigh and scour both the warp and the weft yarns for dyeing in the same dyebath. The Cross+Fire Scarf was dyed using black fiber reactive dye. The resulting color took quite differently on the different fibers. The Tencel weft rendered a true black, while the fine silk weft, which was dyed twice in an attempt to achieve a true black, rendered a deep wine color. The results surprised me, but I took it in stride, as I "speak" ikat and have developed a thick-skinned tolerance for all that can happen in a dyepot. I chose not to change fibers, or rewind and dye a different weft, curious to see how the two dyed colors would pair up when they were woven together and merged as a unified field. This is another example of "The Ikat Rules."

7. WARP AND WEAVE. Dress the loom with the ikat-dyed warp. Don't forget the four warps of copper metallic on each selvedge and the fact that to compensate you should remove four black threads from each side. The warp isn't shifted in any manner; it's simply tied directly onto the back warp beam.

Load your shuttles or bobbins for weaving your weft from the top of the ikat board to the bottom—in other words, backwards. Label your shuttles in the order of weaving.

After weaving in the header material, lay 3 shots of the patterned weft on top and across the patterned warp, and size up the placement situation. Line the warp/weft intersection up just as you'd like it to weave and then assess the selvedges. If the cross pattern lines up nicely but your weft hangs over the selvedges, the warp isn't wide enough and you must add on additional warp threads to make the ikat fit and maintain a beautiful selvedge. If the weft

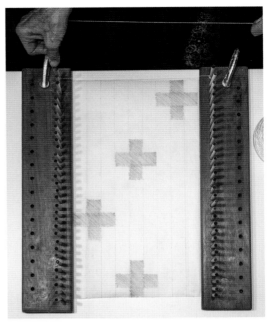

figure 5

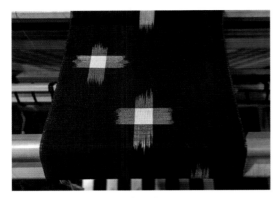

figure 6

completely transverses the warp but doesn't match the ikat warp design when you turn the corner and head toward the other selvedge, your warp is probably too wide, and you need to remove some warp threads.

This fussing doesn't reflect error or mistakes on your part. It's inherent in the exacting processes of weft technique and is very much emphasized in the learning stages. Make the necessary corrections and weave in your weft, lining up the weft and warp intersections and adjusting arcing and bubbling to accommodate the ikat intersections. If your selvedges pull in, the warp is still too wide; simply remove the necessary threads. If the design is nothing but a mishmash of dots and dashes, perhaps you're not beginning the first shot of weaving in the correct spot, or maybe your warp remains too narrow, necessitating adding on more warp.

I understand any discomfort or frustration you might have in making these warp adjustments. This is precisely why most of the world doesn't weave precise selvedge weft ikat, but instead creates elaborate warp-ikat cloth. This also explains why complex double ikats are considered sacred and very precious textiles, now created by a mere handful of families and villages globally.

Once the warp and weft are in agreement with each other, enjoy the process of weaving (**figure 6**). You have a two-phased mission as you do so. The first is to manually control and align warp and weft intersections, arranging them in a pleasing form, and the other is to keep your eye on the selvedges, adjusting the threads so they don't turn a sloppy corner. Double ikat requires that you pay close attention to each shot that you weave. One careless or mislaid shot can throw an entire piece out of design calibration. The reward for all of the measuring, wrapping, dyeing, and fussing will reveal itself as you weave. Weaving and watching an ikat emerge is thrilling and extremely satisfying.

YOKO-KASURI

There are different versions of weft ikat that I don't practice and don't explore in this book. One version is a form of weft patterning mastered by the Japanese, very effective in rendering narrative textile landscapes and pictorial scenes. Beth Ross Johnson has spent decades exploring Japanese techniques for *kasuri*, studying in Japan with ikat masters Jun Tomita and Takayuki Hongo. Her work (see page 13) fluently captures the lyrical nuances of Japanese *yoko-kasuri*. This weft-ikat technique represents another very different point of view and distinct style of designing and weaving resist-dyed threads.

CLOSING WORDS

Weaving is a seductive process. It's tempting to attribute the time invested in the preparation and creation of a piece of cloth as an indicator of its aesthetic relevance. Investing hours is never a substitute for technique and mastery. Allow yourself the time and space to develop artistic content.

Weaving, as all art, is a process that subscribes to a delicate but firm code of ethics. While there are no legal copyrights on plain weave or twill, the making of an indigo vat, or the wrapping of an ikat warp, there is on artistic product. Your responsibility as a student is to adapt all that you've learned into your own unique personal style. Evolve the techniques and treasure the information. Make art and cloth that's uniquely your own.

APPENDIX

HOW TO MAKE A WOODEN STRETCHING FRAME

This DIY ikat-board system, ideal for stretching and wrapping weft ikat, is made with household tools and canvas stretcher boards purchased at an art/craft store, so it requires minimal carpentry skills. It can be assembled in under an hour on your kitchen table. For ease in stretching and wrapping, avoid vertical boards longer than 16 inches (40.5 cm). The width of your project determines the width of the horizontal boards. You can use this frame over and over, replacing the horizontal boards with widths to match your projects.

EQUIPMENT AND SUPPLIES

2 canvas stretcher boards,
   1" (2.5 cm) wider than the project width
   (these will serve as the horizontal boards)

2 canvas stretcher boards,
   14–16" (35.5–40.5 cm) long
   (these will serve as the vertical boards)

ruler

pencil

power drill with ¹⁄₁₆" bit

40 #6 finishing nails

hammer

PROCEDURE

1. Slide the precut stretcher boards into each other to form a rectangle.

2. On each 14–16" (35.5–40.5 cm) vertical board, draw a pencil line centered down the length of the board.

3. Accurately measure and precisely mark ½" (1.25 cm) increments along the pencil line with a dot, centering the holes equidistant from each end of the board. It's important that the dots be aligned directly across from each other on these boards. They will be your nail locations.

4. To avoid splitting the wood with the sharp nails, drill a hole into each dot, or dull the tip of each nail by turning the nail on its head, slightly blunting the tip with the hammer, then use it to make holes.

5. Precisely drive a nail into each of the predrilled holes/dots, embedding the nail deep enough that it won't bend under the tension of stretched yarn, but not so deep as to split the board.

When using, hold the frame on your work table with a C-clamp. This will keep it stationary and make it easier to stretch and wrap yarn.

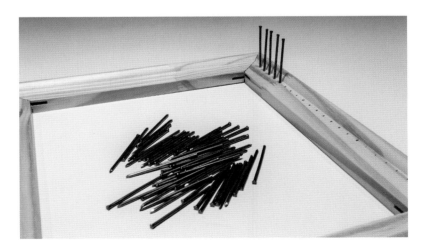

MY FIRST SET OF IKAT BOARDS

My first set of ikat boards were made by a friend in 1986, who had seen something similar in use while on a a woodworking residency in Japan, the land of indigo and ikat. Without question, these boards were the tool for the job. They allowed me to gain more control over my process and develop my ikat skills. I have had dozens of versions of ikat boards made over the years, for teaching workshops and for studio production. This original set remains my favorite, the first boards I reach for when it's time to start wrapping a new ikat.

Each board has 32 small wooden pegs sitting perfectly aligned and spaced in a vertical row. Each removable peg sits in a carefully drilled hole with another identical row of holes drilled alongside the opposite edge of each board (**figure a**). The second row of holes/pegs is used for creating a false tie to extend a section of yarn when wrapping "off the end," allowing you to wrap an entire hank of stretched yarn with no peg interference, creating a total wrapped resist (**figure b**).

figure a

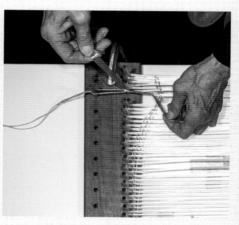

figure b

EQUIPMENT AND SUPPLIES

temporary glue such as Yes Stikflat glue
or Super 77

2 pieces of 1 × 4" (2.5 × 10 cm) pine
or hardwood board, each 18" (45.5 cm) long

ruler

masking tape

¼" (6 mm) drill bit
(a Forstner bit yields the cleanest holes)

drill press or drill

pencil

8 dowels, ¼" (6 mm) in diameter
and 48" (1.2 m) long

sander or loose sandpaper in 120, 180,
and 220 grit

urethane finish (optional)

rag or brush (optional)

rubber gloves (optional)

HOW TO MAKE AN IKAT BOARD WITH REMOVABLE PEGS

This is a project for an experienced hobbyist or carpenter, as it requires carpentry materials and tools.

PROCEDURE

1. Download the template from www.interweave.com/IkatCartoons. Print, assemble, and cut out each of the rectangles in the template as directed in the PDF. Using temporary glue, attach one paper template to the top of each board.

2. Measure up ½" (1.3 mm) from the tip of the drill bit and mark that spot by taping masking tape around the bit. Carefully and accurately drill holes ½" (1.3 mm) deep through the circles marked on the template glued to each board. Accurate ikat registration depends on the accurate alignment of your drilled holes.

3. To create the pegs, measure and cut 99 pieces of dowel, each 3½" (9 cm) long.

4. Sand the ends of each dowel; this will make it easier to insert them into the holes in the boards. Also sand the cut boards; creating a slight, smooth, convex curve along all the top edges will make the boards more pleasant to handle.

OPTIONAL: Seal the boards with a commercial finish while wearing rubber gloves. The parts will be smoother and stay smoother if they get a coat of finish or two, and they'll be less prone to catching or snagging yarns. Sand lightly by hand with 220-grit paper after the first coat.

HOW TO MAKE A WARP-SHIFTING DEVICE

Making this device requires basic carpentry skills and tools. Note that there are many kinds of looms, each with back beams of different angles and dimensions. Be prepared to use trial, error, and a little ingenuity to adapt the device to fit securely onto the back beam of your particular loom.

PROCEDURE

1. Photocopy the template on the facing page at 100%, cut it out, and trace it onto the MDF or fiberboard. Saw it out, and sand the edges smooth so fine warp threads won't get caught or break as they pass across and through the device when it's in use later.

2. Cut a mounting board from a length of 1 × 2" (2.5 × 5 cm) pine, making it slightly shorter than the width of the back beam of your loom. This board will carry the device and be clamped onto the back beam during weaving.

3. Center and align the uncut side of the warp-shifting device flush with one edge of the mounting board. Use two screws to secure it to the mount.

To use the warp-shifting device, place it on the back beam of your loom and secure it using two C-clamps. Adjust as needed so the template lies horizontally, allowing the warp to travel smoothly from front to back of the loom. Figure 1 shows the tool in use.

EQUIPMENT AND SUPPLIES

scissors

pencil

piece of MDF or other high-density fiberboard, same size as design template, ½" (1.3 cm) thick

scroll saw or band saw

sandpaper in 120 and 180 grit

1 × 2" (2.5 × 5 cm) length of pine board longer than the back beam of loom

drill

2 flat-head screws

(2) 3" C-clamps

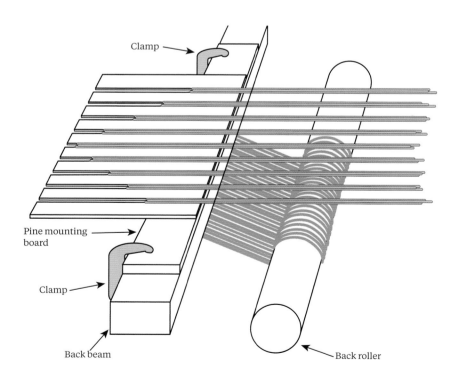

Clamp

Pine mounting board

Clamp

Back beam

Back roller

figure 1

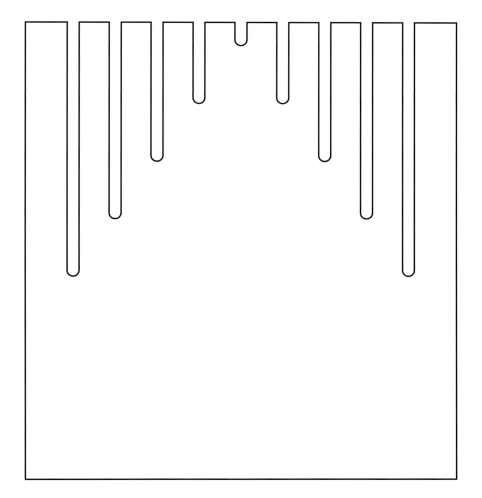

Template for the warp-shifting device.

SUPPLIERS

The fibers, dye supplies, and equipment used throughout this book can be acquired from these sources.

DICK BLICK, www.dickblick.com
Wooden canvas stretcher boards

EARTHUES, www.earthues.com
Indigo and natural dyes

HARRISVILLE DESIGNS, www.harrisville.com
Yarns, looms, warping boards, and raddles

HENRY'S ATTIC, +1-845-783-3930
Natural yarns for dyeing and weaving

MAIWA HANDPRINTS LTD., www.maiwa.com
Indigo, natural dyes and auxiliaries, and resist-wrap ikat tape

NASCO, www.enasco.com
Rolls of paper printed with grids

PRO CHEMICAL AND DYE, www.prochemical.com
Synthetic dyes and dye equipment

SCHACHT SPINDLE COMPANY, www.schachtspindle.com
Looms, raddles, and warping boards

THE LAUNDRY ALTERNATIVE, www.laundry-alternative.com
Mini tabletop spin dryers

WEBS, www.yarn.com
Yarns and weaving supplies

YARN BARN OF KANSAS, www.yarnbarn-ks.com
Yarns, weaving equipment, and supplies

FURTHER READING

The Art and Science of Natural Dyes, Joy Boutrup and Catharine Ellis, Schiffer, 2019.

Central Asian Ikats, Ruby Clark, V&A, 2007.

Colors of the Oasis: Central Asian Ikats, Sumru Belger Krody, The Textile Museum, 2010.

The Dyer's Art: Ikat, Batik, Plangi, Jack Lenor Larsen with Alfred Buhler and Bronwen and Garrett Solyom, Van Nostrand Reinhold, 1976.

Ikat, Lydia Van Gelder, Watson-Guptill, 1980.

Ikat II, Lydia Van Gelder, Unicorn, 1996.

Ikat: An Introduction, Diane Ritch and Yoshiko Wada, Kauri Dyeworks, 1975.

Ikat Fabrics of Orissa and Andhra Pradesh, Bijoy Chandra Mohanty and Kalyan Krishna, D S Mehta, 2017.

Ikat: Silks of Central Asia—The Guido Goldman Collection, Kate Fitz Gibbon and Andrew Hale, Laurence King/ Alan Marcuson, 1997.

Ikat Technique, Jackie Battenfield, Van Nostrand Reinhold, 1978.

Ikat Textiles of India, Chelna Desai, Chronicle Books, 1988.

The Ikat Textiles of Lamalera: A Study of Eastern Indonesian Weaving Tradition, Ruth Barnes, Brill, 1989.

Ikat to Wear, Ankaret Dean, self-published, 1987.

Indian Ikat Textiles, Rosemary Crill, V&A Publications, 1998.

Indigo, Jenny Balfour-Paul, Archetype Books, 2007.

Indigo: The Color that Changed the World, Catherine Legrand, Thames & Hudson, 2013.

Japanese Ikat Weaving: The Techniques of Kasuri, Jun and Noriko Tomita, Routledge & Kegan Paul, 1982.

The Maiwa Guide to Natural Dyes, Maiwa Handprints Ltd., available at www.maiwa.com.

The Modern Natural Dyer, Kristine Vejar, STC Craft, 2015.

Natural Dyes, Dominique Cardon, Archetype Books, 2007.

Patterned Threads: Ikat Traditions and Inspirations, Lotus Stack, Minneapolis Institute of Arts, 1987.

The Techniques of Rug Weaving, Peter Collingwood, Faber, 1968.

Weaving Traditions: Carol Cassidy and Woven Silks of Laos, Dorothy Twining Globus and Mary F. Connors, Museum of Craft & Folk Art, 2004.

The Women's Warpath: Iban Ritual Fabrics from Borneo, Traude Gavin, UCLA Fowler Museum of Cultural History, 1996.

STUDY

Continuing art and textile education and ongoing instruction in weaving, dyeing, and resist-dye techniques is available through these schools and organizations.

ARROWMONT SCHOOL OF ARTS AND CRAFTS, Gatlinburg, TN, USA
arrowmont.org.

HANDWEAVERS GUILD OF AMERICA, Inc., Suwanee, GA, USA
weavespindye.org.

HAYSTACK MOUNTAIN SCHOOL OF CRAFTS, Deer Isle, ME, USA
haystack-mtn.org.

JOHN C. CAMPBELL FOLK SCHOOL, Brasstown, NC, USA
folkschool.org.

MAIWA SCHOOL OF TEXTILES, Vancouver, BC, Canada
maiwa.com.

PENLAND SCHOOL OF CRAFT, Penland, NC, USA
penland.org.

SURFACE DESIGN ASSOCIATION, USA
surfacedesign.org.

TEXTILE SOCIETY OF AMERICA
textilesociety.org.

WORLD SHIBORI NETWORK, Berkeley, CA, USA
shibori.org.

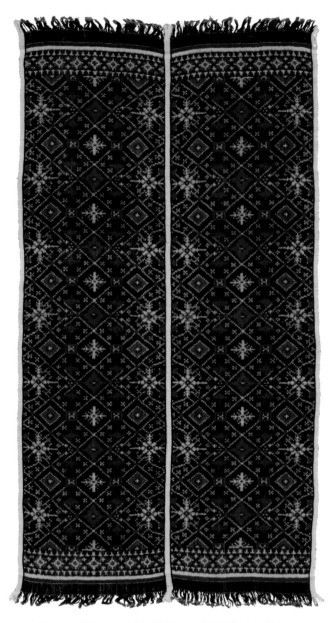

Hinggi warp-ikat ceremonial hip cloth for a man. Ikat by Hiwa Ranja Rudung, dyed by Ngguna Jilik and Tamu Rambu Hamu Eti, woven by May Nggiri, 2006, collection of Ariane de Rothschild, photo: Threads of Life.

INDEX

ACKNOWLEDGMENTS

I dedicate this book to my mother, Anne Mary Hradel Brelowski. You taught me to love the power of the word, the art of the story, and the dignity of simple cloth. In my memory, childhood mornings began at 5:30 a.m. to the tap-tap-tapping of your black Royal typewriter, with you, in your red chenille bathrobe and cup of coffee, firing inspirational missives out to the universe.

I RAISE MY HANDS IN GRATITUDE TO MY TEAM:
Jeffrey Hahn, Paradigm Creative Media, my book process photographer, technology guru, and friend.

Kirby Zicafoose, my exceptional life partner, studio photographer, compass, and rock.

Kale Zicafoose, Tyler Palin, and baby Gray Elizabeth, my precious and priceless trio of happiness.

Anna Dewey Nance, lead studio assistant, visionary, engineer, and saint.

Sarah Kolar, studio assistant, mistress of the dyepots, and master of dependability.

Nathalie Mornu, my savvy, wise, and patient editor.

Catharine Ellis, esteemed weaver of weavers and dyer of dyers, technical editor, and mentor.

And to the many and countless people of cloth—essayists and artists, teachers and students, poets, family, and friends, all of whom have inspired, nurtured, and encouraged me over a lifetime to go where I am led.

Who was it who first convinced me at a very young age that I was an artist? To whomever it was, I believed you. Thank you.

ABOUT THE AUTHOR

Nebraska artist Mary Zicafoose creates woven tapestries saturated with frequency, nuanced with spirit, and technically layered using the timeless process of weft ikat. Her involvement with ikat and archetypal symbols has led her to travel extensively, studying the handwork of weaving cultures that produce ikat cloth.

A passionate artist, teacher, speaker, mentor, and arts advocate, Mary is co-director emerita of the American Tapestry Alliance. Her ikat tapestries are woven metaphors that strive to tie the contemporary, the symbolic, and the timeless together, coded to become powerful emissaries of art and cloth.